THE FIRST
STONE
CAN WE FORGIVE SEXUAL SIN?

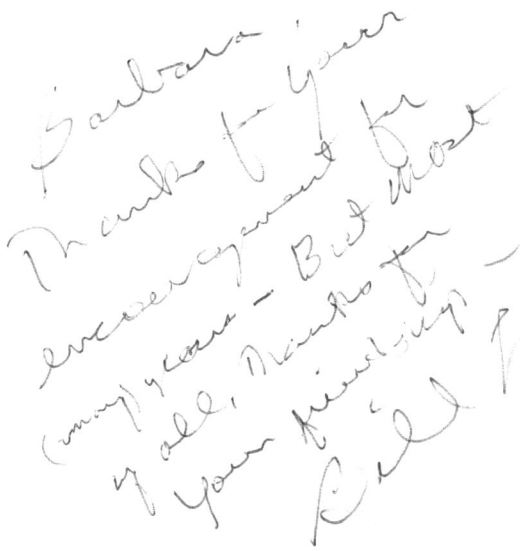

THE FIRST STONE

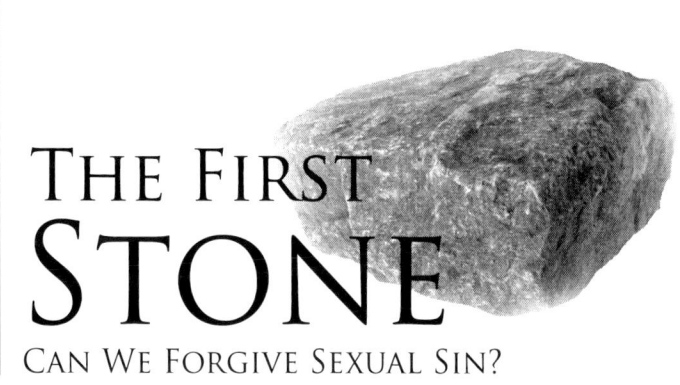

CAN WE FORGIVE SEXUAL SIN?

BILL L. LITTLE, PHD

TATE PUBLISHING
AND **ENTERPRISES**, LLC

Published by Tate Publishing & Enterprises, LLC
127 E. Trade Center Terrace | Mustang, Oklahoma 73064 USA
1.888.361.9473 | www.tatepublishing.com

Tate Publishing is committed to excellence in the publishing industry. The company reflects the philosophy established by the founders, based on Psalm 68:11,
"The Lord gave the word and great was the company of those who published it."

Book design copyright © 2012 by Tate Publishing, LLC. All rights reserved.
Cover design by Lauro Talibong
Interior design by Jomel Pepito

Published in the United States of America

ISBN: 978-1-62147-267-4
1. Religion / Christian Ministry / Counseling & Recovery
2. Religion / Christian Life / Personal Growth
12.11.16

Dedication

To the memory of "Ma" Little
My grandmother who exemplified grace
more than anyone I ever knew

.

ACKNOWLEDGEMENTS

I cannot possibly name all the people who contributed to the writing of this book. I can make special notation of my good friend, Bill Carlin, who read, re-read, and read again the manuscript. He made helpful suggestions and carefully edited the material. I am thankful for his help. Ed Viau read, corrected, and encouraged me. I am thankful for his help.

Thanks to Bob Kenison, of Missouri Baptist Children's Home, who in our brief conversations about this material offered meaningful comments and encouragement.

I am grateful to the many people who have supported me during difficult times in my life. There are too many for me to list here. Suffice it to say, "I am grateful for many gracious and encouraging Christian friends."

TABLE OF CONTENTS

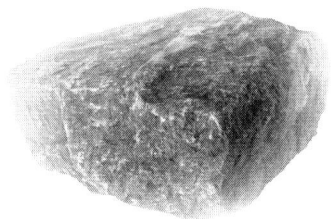

INTRODUCTION

*T*his book is about the transition from throwing stones to spreading grace. It is not about justifying anything but about raising the standard of forgiveness. The strength and size of the grace we give to others is measured by the kinds of things we forgive. Jesus taught that there was no limit to forgiveness and that none of us are qualified to cast the first stone.

I am motivated to write this by the large number of people who are affected in one way or another by sexual misconduct. I know of or have counseled with at least 100 people who have been involved in sexually promiscuous behavior, most in extramarital affairs. There are certainly many people who could be helped by experiencing grace and forgiveness. I will share some of their stories in the opening chapter of this book.

I am also motivated by my own struggles. I have been guilty of failures related to sexual behavior. I have been publicly accused and admit to some truth in those allegations.

I also have had the frustration of dealing with exaggerated charges and misrepresentations. I write because I need to be more open about who I am and trust that I can be a source of encouragement to others in similar situations.

I am also motivated by the hope that by my sharing, others will be influenced to avoid or stop their own misbehavior. The hope is also that there can be a shift in the harsh attitudes toward people who have made such errors. According to studies from the National Opinion Research Center on Extramarital Sex, about 95 percent of Americans say that extramarital sex is wrong, but more than 40 percent admit that they participate. Note that they are the ones who admit such behavior. There are doubtless many more who have been involved, but they are silent about it. It must be clear that there is a difference between expressed attitude and actual behavior. Some of that confusion can possibly be cleared up by material such as this. People often say publicly what they believe is acceptable while not reporting their deepest beliefs and actions.

The lessons here apply to all walks of life and to both sexes and all races. There will be special attention given to the sexual failures of professionals, especially clergy persons. This is an area that surely needs to be addressed. It will be pointed out later that this is an area of failure that is ecumenical. It exists in all religions and to an equal number in non-religious persons. Protestants have been especially critical of the sex scandals in the Catholic Church, but when truth is known, the problem is equally as serious in Protestant circles.

The final motivation is my hope that underlying attitudes and assumptions about people who have sexual failures in their lives can be altered. I will illustrate the importance of accepting, rehabilitating, forgiving, and redeeming such people in the same way that we are able to provide similar actions for people who have failed in other areas of their lives.

When I refer to *failures* in this book, I am referring to moral failures involving sex. I will often simply refer to *failures* because to use the extended statement will be emotionally weighted negatively, and I want to at least lessen the impact of these behaviors. I hope to do that without reducing the standards for morality.

Don't misinterpret what I am saying. I am not embracing the concept that there is nothing wrong with sexual promiscuity and adultery. I hope that is clear when I use the terms misbehavior, misconduct, failure, and sin. If there was nothing wrong with these sexual problems, forgiveness would not be needed. The suggestion here is that sexual sin is no more and no less forgivable than other sins. I am not trying to whitewash anything. My attempt is to be honest, compassionate, and redemptive.

A hint at my attitude is that I wonder how we can accept and commend drug addicts, alcoholics, prejudiced people, convicted felons, arrogant liars, and others who have repented and recovered while not being able to extend the same grace to sexual offenders who have repented and recovered. No matter what you think now, I hope you will be open to examining your attitudes and possibly becoming more understanding and certainly more forgiving.

DEFINING FORGIVENESS

*F*orgiveness is an essential condition for reconciliation (being reunited with someone). I cannot be reconciled to God without forgiveness, and we cannot be reconciled to one another without forgiveness. Forgiveness then tears down the barriers to restoration of relationships. It has different meanings to the forgiver and the forgiven. The forgiver may have concerns that if he or she forgives, or no longer holds a sin against another, then that person will see that as permission to continue the same behavior. Note that forgiveness is not condoning. The forgiven can experience a sense of peace from knowing that there is the possibility of restoration of relationship. That doesn't remove the hurts, the fears, the concerns that any misbehavior produces. The problem is that we all need forgiveness. Place heavy emphasis on *all*. While there is certainly risk involved in forgiveness, there is more risk in not forgiving. Perhaps it will help if we can understand more fully what is meant by *forgiveness*.

The word used most often in the New Testament for *forgive* is the Greek word *aphiami*. It literally means "to send forth, to send away, to lay aside, or to remit." Another word is used in Luke 6:37. It is the word *apoluo*. This word means, "Relieve, release, set at liberty, dismiss, or pardon." When we try to rationalize away the impact of the word *forgive*, we are hard pressed to do so because of the commands of Jesus. Individuals do not have the power in the legal sense to totally forgive illegal actions. We do have the power to remove the barriers actions against us have created in relationships. In that sense we are able to say to offenders, "I do not hold this against you any longer."

Only God can ultimately forgive sins, but we can let go or release people in our lives from the impact of their sins against us. Forgiveness is complicated by degrees of offenses. I can more easily release someone from the impact of a lie than I can from the impact of a murder. Still, if the murderer has repented and served his or her time, I can, by the grace of God, free them from the impact of that behavior on our relationship. This can be complicated further if the murder is of someone close to me, even a child. Even in these cases the power of God to enable forgiveness is often seen. Those cases are often used as evidence of the tremendous power of God in our lives. What is true of love is also true of forgiveness. If we only love those who love us, what more have we done than anyone else? As Christians, more is expected of us (Matthew 5:46-48). I believe the same principle applies to forgiveness.

If we only forgive the "minor" offenses, what more are we doing than anyone else?

Forgiveness has a cleansing and freeing affect on both the forgiver and the forgiven. Whether people accept the teachings of Jesus or not, they would be far better off to exercise forgiveness than to hold onto bitterness, grudges, ill-will, and vindictiveness. An attorney once told me, "If you seek revenge, dig two graves, one for the other person and one for yourself." The teachings of Jesus are practical and healthy for all; still, it is difficult for any of us to practice. That is tragic, especially since we all need to be forgiven. "There but for the grace of God go I."

Stories help us to understand. So I want to share a story that touches my life. I have a friend who is guilty of manslaughter. About ten years ago he killed a woman in a fight when they were both drunk. He is in prison. I visit with him and we often talk of the mistakes he made. We also talk of our hope that he will someday be released and we can again enjoy time together. I find it easy to forgive him because I love him. Would it be different if he had killed someone close to me? Perhaps that is true, but perhaps not.

The mother of the woman he killed has dealt with her grief and has also forgiven my friend. She is on record as supporting a parole for him. The sister of the woman he killed has neither dealt with her grief nor forgiven him. She strongly opposes his being paroled. She is bitter and hostile. The last time I saw her she screamed at the attorney who was seeking to obtain his release. Her feelings and actions will probably assure my friend of spending another ten years in prison and he will, no doubt, die there. His death will not relieve the sister of her grief and anger. I believe the only hope she has for healing is in letting go and forgiving. Note that failure to forgive hurts us more than it hurts the offenders.

Many people oppose paroles and forgiveness unless they are the recipients or unless it is their sons, daughters, spouses, or others whom they love. The fact is that everyone is someone's son, daughter, spouse, or loved one. It is my hope that with more understanding we can all become more merciful in our attitudes. We may never condone offensive acts, but we can set them aside enough to permit a relationship with the offender to exist. That is at least a beginning of forgiveness.

Throughout the following pages I will use the term *forgive* to at the very least mean removing the barriers that separate us from offenders. Be ready to forgive and to accept forgiveness. It is essential to reconciliation between God and us and between one another. The world will never experience reconciliation and peace without forgiveness. Let us pray for the freedom of each of us to forgive one another and to forgive previous generations for all their offenses. I recently read a book, "The Anatomy of Peace," which illustrated reconciliation between an Arab and a Jew. It can happen, but it all begins in our hearts.

DEFINING MISCONDUCT
AND SEXUAL FAILURE

What is this thing called sexual misconduct or sexual misbehavior? Following is an attempt to give at least an elementary definition. The definition is given for clarification. It can be broadened to include a lot of behaviors, but for purposes of this material, it focuses on sexual relationships between adults. Pedophilia is a serious problem that must be addressed, but it is beyond the scope of this book.

Sexual misconduct is a term that is used to describe a variety of situations involving sexual behavior. The definitive description I am using is that it occurs when a member of the clergy, a doctor, employers, or other professionals initiate sexual relations or proposition others for sexual relations.

Sexual harassment has a broader base and includes the making of sexually implicit and explicit remarks to members of the opposite sex, usually in working relationships. There is another category of unethical sexual contact, inappropriate dual relationships, and it especially applies to counselors and clients.

A key difference between misconduct and inappropriate dual relationships is that in misconduct cases an authority figure uses his/her position to seduce or coerce someone into a sexual relationship. State psychological committees, medical committees, and other associations have guidelines that generally apply to the professions that they govern.

The second term, inappropriate dual relationships, covers a wide range of behaviors including socializing with clients. Obviously that would not apply in situations involving clergy. I am familiar with the second term because that term was applied to me after a client's complaint was filed with the state committee of psychologists.

It would be safe to say that misconduct is more serious when one is aggressive in establishing relations with the opposite sex. This might be an important point if legal action is involved. Not initiating the relationship does not remove the ethical responsibility but does change the nature of the offense.

There are many reasons given for infidelity and other unethical sexual behavior, but there is never an excuse. There is rarely a case of sexual infidelity where both participants do not share to some degree in the behavior. Of course there are certain assumptions about this behavior that are made and generalized. There are instances when those assumptions are not totally appropriate. The exceptions will be discussed later, but for now it is accurate to say that in situations of sexual involvement, there is a greater responsibility on the part of authority figures. But this does not mean there is no responsibility on the second party.

It is generally accepted and usually true that greater responsibility rests in people who are in positions of power or authority. A boss involved with an employee is considered more responsible than the employee. A teacher involved with a student is considered more responsible than the student. A minister involved with a parishioner is considered more responsible than the parishioner. A doctor involved with a patient is considered more responsible than the patient. In the military an officer is considered more responsible than an enlisted person or one of lower rank. The list can go on to any situation where there is obviously a difference in authority or power.

It is important to note that there is responsibility of all who are involved in misconduct. Unless we each accept responsibility for our behaviors, we never appropriately deal with them. We carry them deep inside and cannot experience complete healing until we are able to deal openly with our own choices.

There are situations that are brought on through aggressive physical contact by the behavior of the person in the lesser position, but even then there is the assumption (and rightly so) that there is a greater responsibility on the authority or power figure to say no. No matter who initiates the contact, the greater ethical responsibility always falls heaviest on the authority figure. Note that I use the word *heaviest*. In very few cases is there not some shared responsibility. There are degrees of responsibility. A person who is threatened with the loss of job or salary unless they perform sexual favors for a supervisor or boss is less responsible than one that willingly shares in or even initiates the relationship.

The bottom line is that sexual activity outside the normal marital relationship is generally considered to be some form of sexual misconduct. That term is used here as more ethical than legal.

Following are some examples of the behaviors described above.

One example was a client who reported that her doctor had seduced her in his office. She was having issues related to sexual performance with her husband, and the doctor decided to help her by teaching her to use a sex toy. One thing led to another and soon there was sexual intercourse taking place between them. From what I have been told, this is not as uncommon as we would hope.

Years ago a young married woman came to me and tearfully told of an affair she was having with her boss. She had become increasingly uncomfortable with the relationship and subsequently quit her job. Her conflict was generally centered on whether or not she should tell her husband. She chose to accept her own responsibility in the situation and not to tell her husband. She clearly committed herself to never allowing that kind of incident to occur again in her life. The last time I saw her she was still happily married and looking forward to spoiling her grandchildren.

A man came to me for help in dealing with his wife's affair with one of her students in a local high school. She was not really interested in resolving the situation, though he hoped for an opportunity to restore their marriage. That did not happen, and a divorce came. He remains unmarried, and I have lost track of her.

I don't have any idea as to how many ministers have been involved sexually with parishioners. I do know of more than ten specific situations locally. Four of these men came to me for help after their affairs had been made public. Two of them are no longer serving in any church-related capacity. The other two have continued active pastorates. I don't believe there have been repeated incidents with them. I suspect that these four are only the tip of the iceberg in incidents of this nature.

One of the ministers told me that he had been in a miserable marriage for thirty years. He was very open about his decision. He said, "I put in my time, and I am finished with it (the marriage)." He had no desire to restore his marriage, and he had no desire to continue in church-related vocations. He had resigned from his job as pastor of a church were he had served for more than twenty years. In an effort to be encouraging, I asked him if he would like to preach in our church when I was out of town or unavailable. He said, "No, thanks. I don't have any desire to preach any longer."

A second pastor said that he fell in love with a woman in his church, and he divorced his wife. The other woman divorced her husband, and the two of them got married. I spent several hours helping the minister's wife work through her grief in the loss of that relationship.

A third man was guilty of exhibition before young girls. He sought help with the problem, confessed it to the appropriate people, and still serves as an effective pastor.

The fourth was caught in an affair with a young woman from his congregation. His wife refused to even consider forgiving him. I spent time discussing her feelings with her. She was very bitter and did not have any desire for reconciliation. He left the immediate area and still serves in a church.

Two ministers with whom I did counseling were married with families but were sexually confused. Both of them engaged in homosexual relationships. One left his family and lives now with his partner. The other remains in his marriage but still engages in the outside relationship.

A minister from another city said that he decided to divorce his wife and "come out of the closet." He still has regular contact with his children and shares his life with a partner. He still serves as pastor of a church.

My first awareness of sexual misbehavior of a clergyman

My first encounter with ministerial sexual misbehavior came when I was an adolescent. A local pastor was alleged to be involved with a daughter of a prominent family who was also the wife of a teacher. The criticism was harsh, and the man was fired from his job. The woman remained in her job. She and her husband continued normal lives, as far as I could tell. I never understood why the man was fired and the woman was forgiven. I was not against forgiveness but thought it should be equal. Even at that age, I began to suspect that prominence had its advantages. It was much later when I learned that people in positions of authority had greater responsibility (but not all responsibility).

That experience and memory was just a hint of what I was to learn in the future. It was early in life that I understood that ministers and authorities were just as human as everyone else. Still, as I will indicate, there is often imbalance in treatment. There is never an excuse for failing to live up to high moral standards, but that observation applies to everyone, not just the special few.

While there are many professionals able to continue their work even after sexual misconduct, there is really only one profession where members are given a pass. Celebrities are basically exempt from the guidelines that others generally

Bill L. Little, PhD

follow. There is no such exemption for ministers, though
laypeople are equally guilty of the infractions.

In every congregation of which I have had knowledge,
there are people who have been involved in sexual promiscuity
to one degree or another. I have personally dealt with
people who were involved with incest, heterosexual affairs,
homosexual affairs, and struggles with pornography, as well
as a smorgasbord of other sexual conflicts.

I have kept a letter from a young woman in one
congregation who was known to be sexually promiscuous.
She listed twenty-one names of men of all ages who had
either had relations with her or had approached her about
sleeping with them. Seventeen of those men were members of
her church. She was not only confused by all of that but also
very depressed. She made several attempts at suicide. With
help she made it through and in another state married and
raised a family. The most disturbing thing about that whole
story is that I know some of the people she named, and they
have difficulty forgiving others.

That fits with what a seminary professor told one of our
classes. He said that we should be careful of crusaders. They
often crusade as a cover-up to their own problems. When
people are harshly judgmental of others, they may be dealing
with their own guilt ineffectively.

In recent years prominent television preachers have been
involved in sex scandal after sex scandal. I will not name
them, but most readers would easily recognize their names.

Such behaviors are not limited to any one denomination or profession. Several presidents have been linked to sexual impropriety. Athletes, truck drivers, contractors, lawyers, and Indian chiefs—all have been represented in this dubious arena.

My point in mentioning all these examples is to point out that none of us are above the temptation. We are in regular contact with people who are struggling to control their own problems. Still, we seem to act as if these things are not really going on. They are! I believe that we need to generate an atmosphere where people can openly deal with their conflicts and perhaps avoid some of the brokenness that the people I have mentioned have experienced.

SHOULD WE DISCARD
SEXUAL SINNERS?

*T*here was a man who was an outstanding preacher for more than twenty years and led his denomination for several years. There was no question that he had done a good job in both areas. Many thought he probably was instrumental in changing the course of many members of his denomination to a more positive direction. Those who heard him speak thought he was an inspirational speaker and a fine leader. Then it was discovered that for several of those twenty years, he had been involved in an affair with a married woman. He was also married and had a family.

The affair was made public and even spread through the press throughout the state where he lived. He resigned his position with the denomination and is no longer asked to speak anywhere. He was considered a moral failure and looked down on by most people in churches around the state.

His problem is not with God. No matter what the sin, when one repents and asks forgiveness, the scripture says that God forgives (John 1:9). He has asked for forgiveness from people that he offended, especially his wife and the family of the other person involved. Many, including his wife, have forgiven him, but there are many more church people who will not accept him as forgiven and will never forgive him.

I spoke to a friend about the man involved, and my friend said, "I don't understand why no one will permit him to preach any longer." Then he said a very interesting thing. "He was doing what he was doing while he was doing what he was doing. Why can't he be forgiven and do what he was doing for God before the scandal?" That was a good question. It seems clear that God can use any of us, no matter how imperfect we are. Good thing, too.

I responded by saying, "People are not as forgiving as God. It is no accident that there is an oft-quoted statement, 'To err is human. To forgive is divine.'" It is not insignificant that Jesus made so many statements about forgiveness. He made forgiveness mandatory for receiving forgiveness. We all need to be very careful about our willingness or unwillingness to forgive.

Concerning the man mentioned above, some were skeptical, saying, "I wonder if his repentance is genuine? Maybe he is only sorry because he got caught." I respond to that by noting that King David never repented for his adultery or murder until the prophet Nathan confronted him. If one doubts the sincerity of his repentance, read Psalm 51.

It should also be noted that not everyone who is caught repents. I spent time with a man who had been caught in an affair that resulted in the destruction of two families. Before it all came to a conclusion, I asked him what he would say if he stood face-to-face with God and was told by Him to end the affair."

He said, "I'd tell Him the same thing I'm telling you. I will not end it." He didn't.

For me the key for having a forgiving attitude toward a sinner is not *when* or *why* that sinner repented, but *that* he/she repented. Without repentance there is no forgiveness. A wife or husband whose mate has wandered into sexual failure and refuses to repent is a poor risk for future relationship. A mate who does repent at least deserves the opportunity to show evidence of repentance. As hard as it might be for the offended person, forgiveness is the best alterative. In addition there is the fact that in most failed marriages, both mates share at least some responsibility.

Confession and repentance do not change what has happened. In my own experience of personal failure, I am helpless to do anything about my past. When something is done, it cannot be undone, no matter how much we would like that. I would like to undo many things that I have done in the past. I simply cannot do that. My only hope is that I can receive forgiveness from God and from other people who have been hurt, either directly or indirectly by my behaviors.

Do Attitudes Need to Change?

I am asking if attitudes need to change. What I am saying is in no way a justification for sin in our lives. It is an acknowledgement that we all need forgiveness and an observation that some sins are more easily forgiven than others. Lying (at times destroying reputations and influence of a life), prejudice (often leading to unjust treatment of innocent people), hostility and anger (equal in the teachings of Jesus to murder), gluttony (a form of self destruction), greed, envy, judgmental attitudes, gossip, spousal abuse, pride, drug addiction, stealing, arrogance and the like are things that can be forgiven, but it seems that some people view sexual failures to be among the "unforgivable sins" of Matthew 12: 31-32 (NIV).

According to the Bible, no sin is outside the grace of God. "If we confess our sins, He is faithful and just and cleanses us from all unrighteousness" (I John 1:9). I especially am glad that the word *all* is included in this promise. Nothing is outside the forgiving grace of God.

Can Forgiven Sinners Continue to Serve God?

When a person who is a professed follower of God fails, we tend to think he/she should be discarded from ever serving again. This is a mistaken belief.

One dramatic example of God's grace is the life of King David. According to the Bible, David was selected by God to be the king of Israel. He accepted the responsibility and did a pretty good job. Then he got involved with Bathsheba. He was guilty of adultery and, later, murder. He was confronted by the prophet Nathan and subsequently grieved his errors. He confessed and asked for forgiveness. As I indicated above, the depth of his desire for forgiveness is recorded in Psalm 51. He was forgiven and continued to serve as king of Israel. He wrote many wonderful Psalms after these incidents.

Some who would object to forgiveness of sexual misbehavior do so while finding comfort in Psalms written by a sexual failure and a murderer. He had not fallen to the point that he was no longer useful in the kingdom of God.

Perhaps the impact of David's story should be hammered home. Should any of the Psalms that David wrote be discarded? Is it all right to be inspired and comforted by a Psalm written by a confessed adulterer and murderer? What a tragedy it would be to throw away the gifts of this great writer and sensitive soul because of his failures. Still, that is exactly what we do when we fail to forgive similar sins in others who serve.

There is no question but that Simon Peter failed when he denied even knowing Jesus. He was forgiven and became a (some would say *the)* leader of the early church. While not all will agree that the sin of lying about even knowing Jesus is as "bad" as David's sin, surely no one would deny that it was serious. Should we then delete the letters of Peter from the New Testament because they were written after he denied Jesus? Most would say no because he confessed and was forgiven. Does that same standard apply to others?

History is filled with stories of failures and resurrection to service following failures. That is the way God seems to work.

Brennan Manning writes in *The Signature of Jesus*, "There is one spirituality in the church of the Lord Jesus: paschal spirituality. Essentially it is our daily death to sin, selfishness, dishonesty, and degraded love in order to rise to newness of life." When we fail, we die. When we are forgiven, we rise to new life. That is the great news of the gospel.

A Word of Encouragement to Those Who Have Failures

If you have fallen in the eyes of others, do not be discouraged. You can still be raised to life in the kingdom of God. The bottom line is that none of us have fallen so low that we cannot be used by God in His service. We may fall so low that we will not be permitted by people to serve, but our problems are not with God but with people.

The story above is not about me, but it could have been. My own stories are filled with a mixture of wonderful successes in ministry and some terrible failures. I cannot justify my own failures, but I am learning to accept the forgiveness of God and move on.

As I reflect over my own failures and especially the ones that are known by many people, I remember that I have a responsibility for my own actions and must avoid rationalizing any of them and at the same time be willing to go ahead with my life for as long as I can.

Face to face with personal failure, I wallowed in guilt and self-pity. I prayed, asking God how I could go on in ministry knowing now that I was unworthy. After praying such a prayer, I went to sleep. At about 3:00 a.m., I was awakened by a thought that I believe came from God. It was as if a voice in the night said about my concern of now being unworthy, "You, arrogant jerk, you are unworthy. You have always been unworthy. You can continue in ministry as you have before, by grace." It became clear to me that I am never worthy but always live and serve by the grace of God.

Still, I am frustrated by accusations that contain a mixture of truth and falsehood. For instance, a woman who has chosen to exaggerate and misstate what actually happened between us has accused me of sexual misconduct. What happened was bad enough but would not have enabled her to receive acceptance from other people in her life, so the story, as she calls it, has been re-written to cast her in an acceptable light and cast me as a total villain. There is certainly enough trouble with the truth, let alone exaggerated accusations. There is nothing I can do about such a situation. The only hope is to accept God's forgiveness and continue to do the best I can.

It is almost impossible for us not to judge failures. It is probably even more difficult to extend forgiveness when we know someone is guilty. The thing that is often missing is hearing both sides of stories. It is wrong of individuals and professional therapists to make judgments without hearing both sides of stories. They are then better able to sort out facts from fiction and truth from self-serving interpretation.

What I am saying will not make a difference to some. There are arrogant and hypocritical people who will not want to hear that we are to forgive failures in all lives. This especially includes those who see themselves as victimized by our failures. They will do everything that they can to see that those of us who are open failures "get what we deserve." That is tragic. David failed. Simon Peter failed. The apostle Paul said that he failed. All of these people, and thousands like them, continued to serve God after their failures.

Beneath the surface in any congregation of people, leaders included, there is a pool of failures. Sitting in any congregation are people who have had children before marriage and others who got married before their children were born out of wedlock. There are people who are or have been involved in sexual affairs of various kinds. There are closet drinkers. There are liars. There are gluttons. There are all kinds of failures. Still, all of these people have a need for love and forgiveness in their lives. Some of them will never receive that because they are afraid to ever confess and ask for forgiveness. That is a shame.

What happened in my life is that I have been guilty of more things than the accusations of one woman to whom I referred to above, but not with her and not as crass as she described. In the words of the friend I mentioned earlier, "While I was doing what I was doing, I was doing what I was doing." In fact, in the years following my failures and subsequent confession and repentance, I have continued to serve. I have done some of my best work. That might not happen in the future because of what I am writing, but not because of a God problem. It is because of people problems.

I have been re-reading a book written for alcoholics. I almost wish my failures had all been with alcohol. I could start today and live a sober life, a day at a time. For some of us that is possible on an action level. That is, we may not ever have the same failures again, but we cannot be accepted as sober. How in the world can we create a Christian community where all of us failures can be loved and accepted as God's people?

Forgiveness: Don't leave home without it!

No wonder Brennan Manning said, "Forgiveness is the key to everything." If people like me and like many of you cannot be forgiven by people in the church, where are we to go for help? Can we come to you? Is there redemption in the fellowship of the church? And if I cannot forgive you, how will I ever find forgiveness for myself?

My guess is that sexual failure and inappropriate behavior is about the same among ministers as among members of the general population. It is, however, viewed differently because we are supposed to be better than that. I cannot argue with that. Still, a calling does not change our humanity.

Is All Sin In the Same Category?

One of the problems in dealing with this issue is that ministers are not expected to fail. They have excessive pressure on them to at least maintain the appearance of propriety. When they have sexual issues, they are reluctant to seek help. In fact they are frequently reluctant to seek help for any emotional problem.

I saw this as a problem for me and for others in the 1960s. I attended an executive board meeting for my local denominational group and recommended that our association establish a mental health committee, made up of professional therapists who would be available to ministers and their families without charge. After a minister at that meeting voiced the opinion that if people, including ministers, would just read the Bible and pray, there would be no need for such a committee, my recommendation was tabled. So far as I know it is still on the table.

The attitude that all one needs to do is pray and get right with God to deal with emotional and psychological problems has kept many people from seeking needed help. I mention this because ministers would be wise to seek help with personal conflicts, especially those related to family relationships and sexuality. Reluctance to do so can lead to breakdowns in families and in personal life. Unless ministers are free to seek needed help, they are ill equipped to help others with the same issues.

Vital information is needed for ministers of all ages pertaining to the problem of sexual conduct. We evangelicals have been critical of the Catholic Church for not being more open about the sexual conduct of priests, especially in relationship to minors. At the same time, we have often been guilty of mismanaging our own sexual behaviors.

The reasons are fairly obvious. Sins are categorized according to public acceptance. As I indicated above, one may commit a myriad of sins and still be respected for his/her work, but failures in sexual contact have been generally unacceptable. Certainly, no one is justifying misconduct, but there is a need for greater understanding and openness concerning this subject.

To dramatize the need for such information, over the next several pages I will share true stories with only the names changed to protect families and friends of the people involved. I preface these stories with the observation that ministers are no different in their behaviors than others. All of us struggle with our humanness, so I write to inform and not to judge. In fact, I hope this writing will encourage less judgmental attitudes and more understanding.

My first encounters with this issue came early in my own ministry, and I will share some of my struggles and failures later. I was leading a meeting for a small church in Missouri when one of the members informed me that their pastor was involved sexually with one of the married women in the church. I was inwardly very critical of him but decided not to pursue more information about the situation.

Since that time, I have had occasion to deal with a situation where a young pastor sexually exposed himself to some young people in his church. I was brought into the event when I was contacted by a judge who wanted help in getting a confession from him to protect the reputation of the young people who had made the accusation. He avoided further legal problems by admitting the truth. He was not a bad person, but he did a bad thing.

Few of us have not seen the television and other news reports of sexual scandals of prominent religious leaders.

These include pornography, solicitation of prostitutes, homosexual encounters, and assorted affairs.

I know personally of at least a dozen pastors who have been involved in affairs. I have mentioned some of them in the introduction of this material. Most of them have lost their families and their jobs. There are a few exceptions where attempts at redemption through forgiveness have been successful. It seems sad to me that there are not more stories of fallen people who have been lifted up and restored to service. That should not surprise people who are aware that heroes of faith have had such failures and restoration.

Where repentance and forgiveness are involved, it is possible to redeem lives and ministries, but that is a challenging task for most people.

There are several groups that need to be educated in this area. Certainly the goal would be to change misbehavior before it occurs, but the atmosphere must be changed if that is to happen. Ministers need more specific training in dealing with the temptations they will face. Congregations need to be realistic about the problem and at least make some effort at redeeming the lives of those who fail. That can happen if all of us are more open about our struggles.

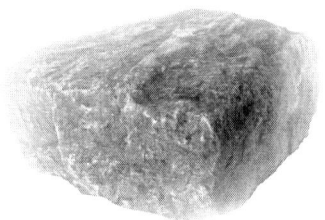

YES, ATTITUDES NEED TO CHANGE

*W*e are wise to remember that people view different errors in different ways. Sexual sins are especially difficult for people to forgive. The following story will help to clarify the reason for this difficulty.

Several years ago I attended a meeting of ministers. The buzz around the meeting was about a minister from a neighboring state who had stolen quite a large sum of money from funds of a children's home. He then left the country.

One man at the meeting said, "That really saddens me. Things like that really give ministers a bad name."

Another chimed in, "Well, at least we can be thankful that he didn't commit an immoral act."

Wow! I thought stealing from money sacrificially given by people, many of whom could not afford the gifts, seemed immoral to me. Taking money earmarked for children without parents and using it to leave the country seemed immoral to me. I realize that what the speaker had meant was, "At least he didn't commit a sexual sin." Sexual sins are not viewed the same as other sin.

It is probably true that I could stand up in front of a congregation and confess to being a member of a hate organization like the KKK or Neo-Nazis and ask for forgiveness, and most congregations would be open to forgiving and might even permit me to preach for them. I could confess to stealing from someone in the church and ask for forgiveness. Most congregations would be willing to forgive. On the other hand, if I stood and confessed that I had slipped into a sexual sin, few if any congregations would be willing to forgive me, and most would not want me to preach in their church. While there is no excuse for such personal failures, there is also no excuse for failure to exercise redemptive attitudes. Christians have often been accused of killing their wounded. Our love and forgiveness must be as large as the sins we confront.

Forgiveness is a key to Christian living. Jesus did not draw any lines. He simply said you must forgive one another. He repeated the idea that if we don't forgive one another, God does not forgive us. Read the eighteenth chapter of Matthew for a strong statement about forgiveness.

One of the greatest challenges for the church and church people, as well as the general public, is to change the underlying attitudes toward sexual sin. This is not to say that there should not be standards to uphold but that we must not forget that all sin falls into the same general category.

Church and Court

My oldest son recently told me that when he is trying a case, especially a murder case, and there has been an indictment by a grand jury, he has to battle, not evidence, but attitudes. Often he enters a case and says that there may be only one person in the courtroom who believes his client is innocent. That one would be his client.

He said that his first challenge is to change the underlying assumptions of guilt. If a judge believes the client is guilty, he/she will be influenced by that assumption when motions or objections are made. We cannot discount our internal belief systems, no matter how hard we might try.

His question for the judge, the jury, and the witnesses, is, "Do you believe my client is guilty (before the trial begins), or do you believe there is a possibility that my client is innocent?" He strives to convince everyone in the courtroom that there is a possibility of innocence. In other words, their underlying assumptions must be brought to the surface in order for a fair trial to be possible. If we can re-frame our belief systems or underlying assumptions, we are less likely to become biased in our decisions.

In sexual misconduct accusations, there is an underlying assumption that this must be the worst conduct imaginable. Anyone who engages in sexual relations outside marriage or commits adultery is a terrible person. I have not found that to be the case. Do you believe it is possible for a good person to be involved in sexual misconduct? If not, you will prejudge anyone who is in that situation. That makes it hard to be accepting and forgiving.

Would your attitude toward sex offenders be different if you believed that this behavior is grounded in misguided love? We assume that sex offenses occur because people are lustful and uncaring. Again, I have not found that to be the case. I know people who have struggled with the problem of sex drive to the point of depression. These are good people with problems. Where are they to go for help? Can they come to your church?

Prodigals and Church

I thought again about the parable of the prodigal son found in the Gospel of Luke, chapter 15. The prodigal son took what his father gave him (not what he earned but what the father gave him) and squandered it in "riotous" living. As the story goes, he was then living in squalor. It was there that he came to himself and decided to go home. He knew he did not deserve to live as a son again but was willing to live as a servant. You know the outcome. He sheepishly returned home and was surprised at the warm and enthusiastic welcome he received.

The story seems to be more about the forgiving father than the erring son. We have all known of fathers who would not have been forgiving at all. The sign on this father's door was *come home*. There are doors that have a different message hanging on them. There are plenty of signs that say, "Don't come home. Prodigals are not welcome here."

There are churches that have welcome signs, and there are others that have rejection signs on their doors. That is true of individuals as well. There are people who have a look of grace on their faces. Prodigals are sensitive to that look. They are also sensitive to the judgmental look on the faces of others. There is no way they want to risk going home to a family or church that is without grace. It is hard enough to take the homeward step after failures even when there is a look of love and grace waiting.

There was a woman who fell into an inappropriate sexual relationship. Circumstances would eventually force her to tell her husband about that relationship. She had lived with him long enough to know that he was an arrogant and unforgiving man. She struggled to find a way to tell him. She knew he would not forgive her if she told him the truth, so she finally came up with a story that he could accept. Of course it was saturated with lies spun to protect her self.

Her lies were accepted, and her husband understood her story. The problem was that her stories brought about tremendous damage to others. She was a prodigal who was afraid to come home. The result was that she compounded her original failure and added lying to the situation. This in turn escalated to hurt even innocent bystanders.

Behind her escalating problems was the knowledge that she was facing an unforgiving husband. Attitudes like his need to be challenged and changed to become more forgiving.

If such attitudes can be changed, marriages can be saved, families held together, and more children will grow up in two-parent families.

Divorce is Not the Only Answer for Unfaithfulness

Another story may make the point even more clearly. The woman in this story is much like the man in the story above. Her husband was unfaithful to her. She discovered the affair and confronted him. He tearfully admitted that it was true and profusely pled for forgiveness. She refused. He continued to plead and beg her to let them begin again. He promised that he would never fail her again. She refused week after week and month after month until finally there was a divorce.

Years later she said of herself, "I was hurt and bitter. I could not or would not forgive him. The children and I have suffered as a result. He later remarried and is living happily with his new wife. I have lived with my bitterness and resentment. If I had it to do over, I would forgive and do my best to have a life with him and our children."

Usually, though not always, it is the unwelcome sign on the doormat of a home, a heart, a church, or a face that turns away the prodigal. The result is that relationships are never repaired and life is lived with the painful results of unforgiving attitudes. The teachings of Jesus are clear and practical: "Forgive one another."

Anyone who is going through the trauma of having an unfaithful spouse, would, in my judgment, be wise to give time for emotions to subside so that a rational and compassionate decision can be made. That decision may be to seek a divorce, but that is not always the best solution.

I personally know of three marriages that have survived unfaithfulness and been restored. All three have more than survived. They have thrived. I think part of the reason is that the erring spouse feels so grateful for forgiveness that he/she works even harder to make sure theirs is a healthy relationship. The forgiving spouse feels good about being able to rise above the failures and honestly accept his/her mate.

There is a negative impact on situations when harsh and negative attitudes are expressed toward the people who have experienced sexual failures: These are attitudes that, fortunately, were not present in dramatic stories from the Bible. Certainly harsh and negative attitudes are not consistent with the life and teachings of Jesus Christ.

The absolutely essential attitude of the church toward all sinners is forgiveness. It must be essential if we base our lives on the teachings of Jesus. In the "Lord's Prayer," Jesus taught that we are to pray that we can be forgiven for our sins in the same way that we forgive those who have sinned against us. At the conclusion of that prayer, Jesus says, "For if you do not forgive others of their trespasses (sins), neither will your father forgive you" (Matthew 6: 15). My forgiveness from God is directly related to my forgiveness of others.

An even stronger statement about the necessity of forgiving others is found in the seventeenth chapter of Matthew. Jesus suggests in this chapter that if we fail to forgive one another, our forgiveness will be rescinded. He said about the canceling of forgiveness to the man who had the great debt but refused to forgive a fellow slave of a lesser debt, "Your Father will do the same to you if you do not forgive one another from your hearts."

We cannot worship or even give our gifts to God unless we have forgiven others of wrongs they have done to us. Jesus said that if we are giving a gift at the altar and remember a situation where we have failed to seek and give forgiveness, we are to leave our gifts at the altar and go seek reconciliation with the person who has something against us. Only following reconciliation are we to return and worship. Forgiveness is absolutely essential for a right relationship with God. Perhaps this recognition will help us to change our attitudes toward those who have been caught up in sinful living. I believe that must include sexual offenses as well as all others.

Accepting attitudes does not mean lowering the standards for behavior. It does mean raising the level of forgiveness. We forgive liars but acknowledge that it is wrong to lie. We forgive thieves but believe it is wrong to steal. We forgive sexual misconduct but believe it is wrong to engage in such conduct. Forgiving murder does not mean we condone killing. The list can go on. We forgive drunkenness, but we believe it is wrong. We even forgive racial prejudice but know it is far short of the standard set by Jesus.

Jesus is the standard for living. We cannot justify falling short of that standard. He is also the standard for forgiveness. We cannot claim his forgiveness without extending it to others. The kind of sin and the magnitude of it in no way affect the actual forgivable nature of it. How can we be forgiven a debt the size of the national debt (and that is considerable) and at the same time not forgive one who is late in payment of a bill for a month's rent? Lying, racial prejudice, stealing, arrogance, pride, and the like are just as responsible for the sacrifice of Jesus as murder and adultery. While I am urging forgiveness for the latter, I am also advocating forgiveness for the former. Grace is the only hope for any of us. None of us are worthy of God's grace; that's why we call it grace.

The Shack is a fictional story about a man's struggle to forgive the person who murdered his little girl. The story goes that Mack, the father of the murdered girl, says that he doesn't want to forgive the murderer. He wants him to suffer and experience pain as he has. He is challenged by the presence of God to forgive the man and let God redeem him. When Mack reaches the place where he can forgive, he becomes free of the burden of pain that he carried with him and experiences peace. The story may not fit your theology, but it will fit your life, and it fits the teachings of Jesus.

This is more than a fictional story. It is about us all. The depth of our spiritual strength is measured by the size of our forgiveness. One of the most impressive experiences of my life came when my friend, the late Lee Dodd, called me in the middle of the night with the shocking news that his youngest daughter had been killed in a wreck caused by a drunken driver.

I met Lee and his family at the county hospital and later traveled with him to a hospital in the city. We got on the elevator to go get the body released and there Lee said to me, "Bill, let's pray for the man who killed Jan. He will have to live with that for the rest of his life." That is Christian grace!

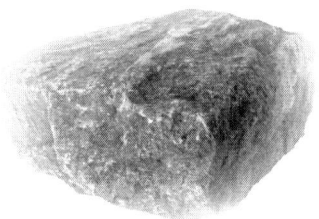

EMBRACE GRACE

*O*nly people who understand and express the grace of God will be open to change in their attitudes toward fallen people. When we attempt to change attitudes toward sin and sinners in the church, we will be forced to face entrenched legalism that leaves little or no wiggle room. As defined by Wikipedia, Christian legalism is "a sometimes pejorative (derogatory) term referring to an over–emphasis on discipline of conduct, or legal ideas, usually implying an allegation of misguided rigor, pride, superficiality, the neglect of mercy, and ignorance of the grace of God or emphasizing the letter of the law over the spirit."

The Scribes and Pharisees were clearly legalists in their religion. They emphasized obedience to the Law of Moses to the letter without understanding the concept of grace. The attitude produced by that approach to morality is perhaps best illustrated by the story of the woman who was caught in the act of adultery.

Legalism demanded that she should be stoned to death. Jesus ignored that demand and challenged the one who was without sin to cast *the first stone*. No one did. When they left, Jesus asked her who was there to condemn her. When she said no one, Jesus said, "Neither do I condemn you. Go and sin no more" (John 8: 1-11). Legalists kill rather than forgive.

It is the attitude grounded in grace that was expressed by Jesus that is absent in legalistic religion. I believe that legalism (in religion) is an attitude and mindset that seeks to control others through authoritative laws. The laws are usually said to come from God, or to at least be inspired by God. The idea is to intimidate people who may disagree.

Religious legalists will resist forgiving people who have committed any sin but especially any who have committed a sexual sin. They do not want such people to be restored to their places of service. Grace is too risky for them.

The real demon is the idea and the attitudes produced by the idea. It is the ideology that is the real culprit. Before you embrace an ideology, take a look at what it leads to. Never get on a plane if you don't know where it is going. Several years ago I boarded a plane in Fort Smith, Arkansas. We were headed for St. Louis. When the plane began to taxi toward the runway, there was a loud banging noise coming from beneath the plane. In a few minutes, the pilot announced, "One of the baggage handlers got closed into the baggage compartment. He doesn't want to go to St. Louis today, so we have to turn back and let him out." If the plane is not going where you want to go, don't get on board.

Over the years in my own ministry, I have persisted in attempting to demonstrate the destination of legalistic theology. If strongly adhered to, it becomes harsh, judgmental, and mean-spirited. I don't want to go there! Legalists seem to be driven by the desire for authority that will give them a sense of security. Ultimately that search is shipwrecked on the shores of reality. There is no security outside our faith and the grace of God.

We all need to remember that we have among us people who can also become harsh and mean spirited. Human frailty doesn't die because we become people of faith, moderates, liberals, or otherwise. Remembering that will help us to maintain a little humility, but it must not stop us from speaking out. I know that I often forget compassion when I am faced with legalism. I become my own enemy in those situations. I want to be a forgiving person.

It is difficult for us to grasp the necessity of grace for our own redemption. It is my contention that I am saved by the grace of God, not by any works of law that I might do (Ephesians 2:8-9). That is a cardinal principle for those who want to become more accepting of sinners and more willing to extend personal forgiveness to people who may have offended them or violated moral laws. Nothing is beyond the forgiveness of God, and no one is beyond His redeeming grace.

If you are a legalist, you will find it hard to sing with gusto, "Grace, grace, greater than all my sin." Or perhaps it is more likely that you will have trouble singing, "Grace, grace, greater than your sin."

One of the lessons I learned about grace came to me from an unexpected source. I had lunch with one of my graduate school professors. My first book was doing well at that time. She asked me how it was doing. In retrospect I realize my answer was a feeble attempt at humility. I said, "It is doing better than I deserve."

Her response surprised me. She said, "Deserving doesn't have anything to do with it." That comment reverberates in my head to this day. A common mistake I make, and I suspect many others make, is in believing that I earn or deserve good things from God. I don't. I am always in need of grace.

Pious people in general and staunch legalists in particular seem to forget that we are all in the same boat. The old spiritual song has it right. "It's me. It's me, O Lord, standing in the need of prayer." We can substitute the word *grace* for the word *prayer*, and we are stating reality.

If our attitudes can be raised above legalism, we can invite all the broken humanity around us to lift up their heads. Neither do we condemn you. Go and sin no more.

PREVENTION IS THE GOAL

*E*ven if we are successful in changing attitudes, we still have to face the need to resist all inappropriate behaviors. People can learn to accept us even though they disapprove of our actions. It remains our responsibility to find ways to prevent making the same errors in the future. Following are some suggestions that may help prevent future failures.

As in the illustration above about destinations, looking at the end of a behavior before it is done can be a deterrent. Stephen Covey in his wonderful book, *The Seven Habits of Highly Effective People*, says, "Begin with the end in mind." That requires some practice. Reason may become short-circuited in the heat of a moment. We would all be wise to practice saying to ourselves, "Before I do this, I want to know where it will lead." Careers and lives have been thrown into chaos because of decisions and actions that took place in a moment of passion.

I once asked Dr. Burkett (an oncologist from England) why prevention was not practiced more in managing disease. He said, "It doesn't pay as well as treatment. You Americans seem more interested in mopping up water than in turning off taps." A lot of heartache could be avoided by turning off the faucets. Looking before you leap is easier said than done, but it is a vital habit. That is certainly true of sexual encounters.

Boundaries of all kinds

On a personal note, I will tell you that as a young minister I was given warnings about women who would tempt and test my moral commitments. I knew that this was possible but had no idea how widespread this problem was. I was told to not visit female parishioners alone in the home. I was told to not meet with female parishioners behind closed doors alone. I was told not to give a ride to a female parishioner alone in my auto.

These guidelines are protective measures that were recommended to me early in my ministry. I saw them as unreasonable and unnecessary. I still believe that is true but partially because they only protect people who probably do not need to be protected. If one wants to behave improperly, he/she can find a way.

It seems to me that boundaries that best serve us are boundaries of love, respect, and reverence. If we love people, respect people, and reverence people, we are not likely to be improperly involved with them. The same boundaries apply to our selves and to God. Love, respect, and reverence yourself and God. This guideline includes the great commandment, to love God and to love others as you love yourself.

I saw these as overreactions and hindrances to my freedom to minister to needs. I saw no reason to exercise such extreme caution. These legalistic guidelines are overkill and often artificial. I have not had problems with giving a ride to someone who needed one, even a member of the opposite sex. But I suggest to any young minister that he or she take seriously precautions about relationships with the opposite sex. Here are some true stories that clarify the problem.

Similar stories could be told concerning practically every profession, but I have special interest in communicating with ministers and especially young ministers. I wish that every young seminarian would read these accounts and take note.

Prevention could have saved the ministry of the man in the story that follows.

A minister whose life and ministry were impacted terribly recounts this story. He visited a woman who had called him to come to her home when she was ill. He was shocked when she met him at the door wearing a flimsy negligee. He quickly came up with an appropriate response, "I'll leave and give you time to get dressed. I'll come back in about an hour."

He said that he was pleased with his wisdom in handling the situation and was confident that he could handle going back to visit with her. Reminds me of the thing about pride and a fall.

He did return, and this time when he rang the doorbell, she opened the door but stood behind it while he walked in. She then stepped out and was wearing less than she had worn before. He did not handle this situation as well as he thought he could. When she walked to him, they wound up on the couch and one thing led to another. He left feeling like a fallen man. He just didn't know how far he was about to fall. The woman shared the event with her neighbors, and news spread quickly back to his congregation. They were not the kind that would give him another chance. Many people find it almost impossible to forgive sexual failures. I restate my opinion that there are no failures that should be outside the realm of forgiveness. This is certainly true for Christians.

That whole incident could have been avoided if the minister had observed stricter boundaries. Prevention occurs when we recognize our own limitations and when we observe reasonable boundaries. It also occurs when we consider the consequences of a behavior before engaging in it.

Physical boundaries

What about a back rub? Often, what appears to be a harmless behavior can lead to harmful behavior. An innocent back rub can turn into inappropriate touching and a great deal of conflict. I have learned the hard way that boundaries must be set and observed. There was a time when I thought setting a boundary of not touching a client or allowing them to touch me was artificial and legalistic. I now know better. Perhaps the old adage is correct, "We are too soon old and too late smart."

I know of a situation where a woman offered to give a man a back rub. Whether that was an innocent action, I cannot judge, but I can tell you that it was inappropriate. That led to inappropriate touching that went on repeatedly until it was out of hand. Truth is that it was out of hand from the time of the offer of the back rub and his lying down to accept the massage. In that situation there was never a consummation of sexual intercourse, though they came very close once. Her recollection of the events has grown over the years and evolved in her telling her story to as many people as would listen.

This series of events led to tremendous hurt, not only in the families who were directly involved but also in the many people who were dragged into the situation by what I believe was the vindictiveness of the victim, who believed she had psychological and ethical absolution and had absolutely no culpability for any of her actions. The point to sharing this is to wave a red flag in front of anyone who is tempted to toy around with physical contact with the opposite sex. It can only lead to disaster.

Spiritual boundaries

Becoming too intimate in sharing, even personal prayer times, has led to affairs of the heart. It is difficult for people to share their inmost thoughts for long periods of time without becoming tempted to share more than intimate thoughts. I know of specific situations that have evolved from well-meaning relationships of that nature. One such relationship led to the divorce of both people involved. I hope that a word to the wise is sufficient.

In an article from the *Journal of Marriage and the Family* from 1984 the following observation was made. "The strongest predictor of permissive attitudes on extramarital sex for men and women is the ability to share one's most personal and intimate feelings with persons other than one's spouse." Caution really must be exercised when we share intimate thoughts with one another.

I know of long-term affairs that began with intimate sharing that included regularly praying together. It is amazing how easily a spiritual intention can be turned into a physical attraction. There may be no interaction that makes one more vulnerable than sharing intimate thoughts and feelings in prayer.

If you are not taking seriously what I am saying, please note that once the label of sexual misconduct is tacked on to a person, it is nearly impossible in our culture to move away from the implications. The place to stop that is in the drawing of boundaries and exercising caution.

I know that what I am writing is true. I have made tragic mistakes in judgment and in behavior. The result is that I have been accused of inappropriate relationships. Allegations have been made against me, some true, but thankfully most were not true. I have confessed to improper touching and been devastated by the exaggerated stories that grew out of that. I am fortunate to have had many wonderfully supportive Christian friends to help me through. At the same time, I have experienced the bitterness and hostility of unforgiving people, as well.

Thank God for compassionate and understanding people in the lineage of Jesus Christ. I need them, and I need His mercy and grace in my life every day.

As hard as it might be for some to believe, the lowering of boundaries in order to give spiritual support and comfort to grieving people has on many occasions led to the development of affairs. It is certainly acceptable to give an encouraging hug to a person who is in the throes of grief. It is wise to do that in the presence of others. It is a shame that such touching, often sorely needed, is unwise.

I learned that lesson in an embarrassing situation. I was counseling a rabbi and his wife. She became distraught during one of our sessions. She was sitting in a chair that was between the rabbi and me. I instinctively reached out and touched her hand. He became quiet and later in that session he said, "In our faith (orthodox Judaism), you are never to touch another man's wife." I apologized, and we continued the session.

It seems to me to be extreme, but it is better to err on the side of safety. I do believe there are exceptions to these guidelines, but in general it is better to avoid physical contact in highly charged emotional moments.

EMOTIONAL BOUNDARIES

*S*haring intimate details of our lives with one another is important if there is a positive purpose for that sharing. It is wise to exercise care in sharing intimacy just for the good feelings we get from such sharing. When it leads to an observation that "I can't share like this with my spouse," a dangerous line is crossed. There are limitations.

Obviously risks must be run when we are helping people deal with emotional pain in their lives. The more mature we are, the freer we are to run some calculated risks that may indeed be healing to others. Just don't overdo.

One of my favorite lines from a Clint Eastwood movie is, "A man has to know his limitations." We need to know our own limitations and keep them in mind.

Don't be surprised

Read this material to equip yourself for what can happen. When I was a young man, I received some good advice from an older friend. On a trip we made together, he would have me look down the road and guess at what could happen with oncoming traffic. He said, "Learn to drive defensively. Anticipate what might happen and think about what you can do to deal with that."

I am saying that we can learn to live defensively. As you read the stories in this material, look at them as approaching traffic. How would you handle situations like these? In my fifty-plus years as pastor of one church, I have heard just about every kind of story you can imagine. I am not a priest, but I have heard a lot of confessions. Too often I thought about how I should respond to the people involved. I have not condemned or judged any of the people who have shared with me. I have tried to encourage them to pray for forgiveness and have assured them that I have no trouble forgiving them. I have not shared any of their experiences with others and will not do so now.

What I failed to do was to see the events as warnings for me. I never, or seldom, asked myself how I would respond in similar circumstances to those of the people who were sharing with me. I have learned very late in life to live and drive defensively. My wife and children are not sure about the driving part, but I have learned to live defensively.

Being prepared is a vital part of prevention. Even so, there will be unexpected things that will throw you. Learn to pause between the stimulus and your response. In the pause ask yourself, "How do I want to respond to this situation?" You will always have a choice. Read on and pause as you read these examples and imagine how you could best respond in similar circumstances.

It can be flattering to have someone wanting to be in our presence. That can become unhealthy. There are times in my experience and to my knowledge where a woman has literally stalked a therapist, minister, or boss. The same is true of men stalking an authority figure in their lives. In one case, a woman was in a counselor's office every time he finished a session. She wanted to know if he had time to meet with her. She called him regularly. He finally agreed to see her but not professionally. When the relationship did not work out to her satisfaction, she sued him for an inappropriate relationship. I do not know the outcome of the lawsuit.

Once a young prostitute sought counseling help. I am told that at the second session she told the therapist that she would be a lot less nervous if they had sex. He wisely said, "That might be true, but it would make me a lot more nervous." We all need to be ready to appropriately confront difficult situations with wisdom.

Review other stories I have shared in this material and imagine how you would best respond. Preparation is a preventive.

Think about consequences

If you find yourself in a tempting situation, think about the consequences of involvement in a sexual affair or any other temptation. Here is a short list of possible consequences to sexual affairs:

Guilt: If you are like more than 95 percent of the people in this country, you believe that sexual affairs are wrong. That underlying belief will affect you in the future. If you are married, you will think of what you have done when you look at your spouse and other members of your family.

Fear: On some level people who feel guilt are afraid of being exposed. *What if my friends find out? How can I keep a lid on this? How do I know the other person will not talk to others about it? What will happen to me if my spouse finds out? What will happen to me if people at my work find out?* Such questions produce fear that will be expressed in stress.

Collateral damage: Others will be hurt by our bad behaviors. This is most obvious in families where there are children. If an extramarital affair takes place and results in a stressful atmosphere at home or leads to divorce, the lives of children will be scarred.

Broken spiritual relationships: Though God will forgive us when we sin, we still have to deal with the idea that on some level we have failed. It takes a while for us to feel normal again. We are all hypocrites anyway, so when we add a specific sin and try to go on with our spiritual lives, we feel even more hypocritical. We simply do not feel as close to God as we know we should. Whether that is a fact or feeling, it still affects us.

Jesus said that it is unwise to begin to build without considering the cost (Luke 14:28). I am focusing on sexual sin, but the principles apply to all sin. Before getting drunk, consider the cost. Before risking your earnings in gambling, consider the cost. Before taking drugs, consider the cost. Before spreading gossip, consider the cost. Before engaging in sexual misbehavior, consider the cost.

Strengthen your own relationships

Perhaps the greatest prevention of sexual promiscuity in the world for married people is the strengthening of their own relationships. When we learn to respect, love, and reverence the people in our lives, we will certainly not be inclined to look for other relationships.

It is easy to forget those closest to us. A physician's wife told me, "I wish he cared as much for me as he does his patients. I just wish he would give me a hug when he comes home."

A minister whose family was falling apart paced the street in front of his home. He was heard saying, "I have cared for the flocks of others but have left my own untended." Focusing on our own families will resolve a lot of potential problems.

Remember that it is easier in the long run to turn off the faucets than to mop up the water. Prevention is still the ultimate cure.

SEXUAL SIN IS
ECUMENICAL AND
FORGIVABLE

*T*he Catholic Church has been criticized for not being harsher in the treatment of priests who have molested young men. It should be noted that when this behavior involves young children, it is not only unethical but also illegal. Certainly those involved must be confronted, and the behavior can never be condoned. This will be hard for some to accept, but I believe that even such heinous behavior as theirs can be forgiven when there is genuine repentance. All of us rely on the grace and mercy of God.

I know that some of the priests who have admitted their abusive behavior are being "treated" in special programs. Some are critical of the careful way these people are handled, but we need to remember that none of us are so bad that God cannot use us if we are willing to be used.

Do not misunderstand what I am saying. I am not justifying any of these abuses. I have seen the brokenness of a wife and children left by a husband who left them because of his involvement with another woman. I have this very day met with a woman who is struggling with the break-up of her daughter's marriage and the devastation it has brought to the children in that family.

Churches are divided. Families are destroyed. Careers are ended. Suicides take place. Scars are left on children for the rest of their lives. All these things happen because of sexual misconduct and failure. I hasten to add that other moral problems such as racial prejudice and ensuing actions of hate crimes have also divided churches, destroyed families, and left children scarred for the rest of their lives.

I re-emphasize that socially acceptable sins can be just as devastating as the less acceptable ones. Gossip is an example of one of those sins. Loose lips have ruined lives. Most of us have seen the pain and havoc left in the wake of, "I don't know if you have heard this or not, but I heard that—" Can we forgive prejudices and gossip? These are just two in a long list of devastating sins.

Sin is an equal-employment activity. One of the reasons we need to maintain a compassionate attitude toward sinners is that we are some of them. None of us, regardless of denomination, race, creed, profession, or nationality, are free from temptation and the possibility of failure. I know that I have failed in many ways.

I have committed many sins in my life. I have cheated on the golf course. Sometimes I have been the one who hits a Wilson ball into the rough and finds it, then hits the Callaway out of the rough. I have even forgotten my exact score and reported a slightly lower number. I have copied some answers on tests. I have stolen a few items from places of employment. I have lied about my involvement in embarrassing situations.

A teacher once called me on the carpet because I had crawled under a frame school building. There were five boys and at least an equal number of girls who participated. I got the boys together, and we made up a story saying that the girls crawled under the building and called us to follow them, but we only went to the edge and looked under the building. We all stuck to our story, and the girls were punished while we "innocents" were just given a warning. I have been guilty of defacing public property. I have treated some people unfairly. I have gossiped, even when it was damaging to others. I have been drunk once and often obnoxious.

In all these things and many similar things, I have been guilty but have always been forgiven by good people, including Christians. But, when I slipped up sexually, the forgiveness has not been as freely expressed. Most of my closest friends have been understanding and forgiving, but many others have not been willing to do that. This is not the unforgivable sin that Jesus mentioned. In everything except sin against the Holy Spirit, he commanded forgiveness. There are no exceptions.

Manning on forgiveness

Consider this. "The most characteristic feature of the humility of Jesus is his forgiveness and acceptance of others. By contrast, our non-acceptance and lack of forgiveness keep us in a state of agitation and unrest. Our resentments reveal that the signature of Jesus still is not written on our lives. The surest sign of union with the crucified Christ is our forgiveness of those who have perpetrated injustices against us" (Manning, *The Signature of Jesus*). Failure to forgive will leave us with troubled hearts and restless nights. Surely we need no more dramatic example of the spirit of Jesus than his cry from the cross, "Father forgive them because they don't know what they are doing."

Even a casual reading of the gospels will bring the message of Jesus on forgiveness into focus. It is one of the clearest teachings of Jesus. We must forgive or we cannot be forgiven. (Read the Sermon on the Mount and Matthew 18 as examples.)

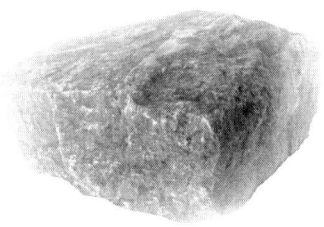

SOME RELATED CONCERNS

Attitudes toward people who are accused

*B*ear in mind that it is easy to accuse someone. The accuser usually has the advantage of telling a story first and putting his/her own spin on it. Few people will tell a story on themselves that is incriminating. They don't mind incriminating someone else, especially if that person has disappointed them or hurt them. It then becomes easy for those who hear the story to assume that the person who came forward is acting in good faith. "Why else would they share embarrassing events?" Why? Because in many cases it gives them a chance to justify themselves and condemn the other person involved.

The fact is that there is seldom an innocent person in a sexual affair. Usually there is plenty of responsibility to go around. That responsibility frequently reaches outside the immediate people involved. It may involve a spouse or other person who has participated in provoking the behavior. This in no way excuses either party, but it does at least add some understanding to the situation.

Our attitudes would be healthier if we held off on making judgments until we had more information. In almost all cases, we simply do not know enough to make judgments. In general do not assume too much. Refer back to the discussion of "church and court." Assumptions make it difficult for us to be objective.

Attitudes of People Who Have Been Involved in Sexual Relationships Outside of Marriage

Empathy for people and acceptance is vital if we are to be instruments of healing and redemption for such people. Examine your own attitude before attempting to help someone deal with such problems. At least hold off on making judgments.

It is often difficult to determine the truth in situations where there are different accountings of the story. Memory can be hazy and remembered in different ways. One of the ways some of us test our counseling success is by comparing the early recollections of a client when they first come in with a presenting problem with the way they remember the same events after counseling has been done. When the person begins to see himself differently, he will remember his past differently. Legally it is well known that eyewitness testimony is highly unreliable. Corroborating evidence is required. That is usually not possible in the he-says-she-says stories of sexual encounters.

Certainly, long-term memory is suspect.

In the case of ministers, it is the parishioners who experience a huge amount of pain. In one case with which I am familiar, a woman accused a minister of sexual misconduct with her. In doing so she told as many people as she could about her accusations. She even wrote a number of letters informing members of that church about her alleged experience.

The pastor had developed close relationships with many of the people in that church. They were devastated and confused. They loved the man but didn't know how to deal with the situation. They needed pastoral ministry but were reluctant to ask the pastor for his help. That was true when there were serious illnesses and even deaths to face. Their ability to get help was not only damaged by the failure of the pastor but also of the constant barrage of accusations they faced. Some collateral damage could be avoided with less talk.

People outside the fellowship of churches look at such situations and decide that there is no point in looking for spiritual direction from people who are obviously experiencing failure in their lives. The fact is that we all have failures in our lives, whether we are in church or not. It is just tragic that our failures fall on people who could have used our help in facing their own struggles.

If people of the world could see more forgiveness and redemption in churches, they would be more likely to risk seeking help for themselves.

Hope for those who have failed

You and I have the same hope that everyone has. We have hope for forgiveness and redemption in the grace of God. I have written this with the prayer that it will keep someone from falling, and if one has already fallen, it will help him/her to get up again.

If you are among the fallen, there are several things that you need to remember. First, remember that nothing you have done is outside the forgiveness of God. So don't waste life by wallowing in guilt. Confess, repent, and ask for forgiveness, then move on. Guilt is essentially a useless emotion. "Don't take a guilt trip. Take a trip to the mall, even to the next county. Travel to a foreign country, but not to where the guilt is" (From an Internet article on healthy aging, "Ten Tips for Staying Young"). The only real justification for guilt is, "If something is going to make you feel guilty, don't do it."

Second, remember that you are loved. One thing that is surer than death and taxes is the love of God. The book of First John is filled with promises of God's love, based on the fact that God is love. Whether you know it or not, there are people who love you. I am often surprised by the strength of a Christian friend's love. You are loved!

Third, you can live a normal life again. Failures of any kind are simply bumps in the road that are overcome by grace. I love a comment made by Brennan Manning, "No one has sunk so low that he cannot be used by God." That came to me at a time when I was really struggling with my own lack of self worth. Find something that you enjoy doing and begin doing it. I have not many opportunities to preach these days, but I thoroughly enjoy writing. I believe some of the things I write can be useful in the lives of readers.

Fourth, there are plenty of good things going on in your world and in the world around you. Every day that you are above ground and sucking air is a day to give thanks. I thank God for each day before my feet hit the floor in the morning. Start giving thanks in everything, and you will be amazed at the peace that begins to fill your life.

So stop treating yourself poorly. Think of the things you would love to do for and say to someone who is in a situation like yours. Do and say those things for yourself. We are to love others as we love ourselves.

One more observation is important. If you have the good fortune to have friends, family, coworkers, employers, or churches that give you a second chance, be sure to do everything in your power not to fall again. Thank God for second, even third chances, but don't continue pursuing bad behavior and bad habits.

Making good on second chances will be made more probable if we remember our value.

We are all human beings struggling to live. We do different things in life, but we all have equal value and importance, both in the kingdom of God and in this world. What we do can be good or bad, but that has nothing to do with our value. We have value simply because we are human beings. Over the years I have found that everyone needs to know that fact. It is encouraging, and the knowledge of it often helps people overcome some of the problems they face in life.

One example may help to clarify this principle. I have worked with alcoholics, cancer patients, and just about everyone in between. I usually gave each one an assignment. Memorize the following statement before our next meeting. "I have as much worth and value as anyone in the world. I don't have to earn it or prove it. It is mine because I am a human being, created by God. I have as much worth and value as anyone in the world." That is a wonderful statement for anyone to memorize and repeat.

The fact that you have had failures in your life doesn't mean that you are a bad person. Bad people do good things, and good people do bad things. I just think that many of us do not remember that good people get caught up in sins of passion. I wonder why they don't just confess their sins and ask for forgiveness? Perhaps it is because they know they have been pre-judged by the other good people. I have often prayed, "God save me from the good people. They can really hurt us." Sexually scarred people are asked by the good people in the church to fall on their swords as an act of cleansing. That is an unfortunate and evil way to approach sinners of any kind. Redemption is the first goal of Christians, not judgment and condemnation.

Forgiveness in: Divorce out

I mentioned earlier that divorce is not the only option when failures have occurred in marriage. When married couples are facing the crisis brought on by unfaithfulness in their marriages, a multitude of emotions and reactions surface. Most of the emotions and reactions are grounded in ego. Think of the words: "How could you do this to me? I have never been so hurt in my life."

First reactions may be expressions of personal pain that evolve into anger and bitterness if unchecked. Seldom are there thoughts of forgiveness and restoration. If children are involved, they are secondary to the personal thoughts. Too much of our focus is on ourselves.

The point I have been trying to make throughout this material is that we can choose to exercise the option of forgiveness and that is essential to reducing the pain for all involved. Just like businesses, churches, political groups, and others, families face the choice of throwing the guilty person out and sacrificing all the good that could come from restoration or forgiveness.

The decision to discard a marriage, especially when children are involved, is complicated by the stress placed on the children. If they are old enough, they will face choices like: "Where will I live?" "Which parent will I choose?" "Whose fault is it?" The fact is most children have less trouble forgiving a misbehaving parent than they do dealing with a divorce.

There are plenty of reasons for saving relationships. These certainly include what is best for the children. Of course in some cases the marriage has devolved into a barren relationship long before or during the affair that occurred. In those cases there are seldom any benefits to staying together. But if there is still the possibility of rebuilding, children will do better with two parents and so will the mates.

I have a bias in favor of saving marriages. I know that there are some relationships that have deteriorated to the point that they are destructive to the people involved, but those are exceptions. Most divorces could be avoided with patience and effort on the part of both partners to work on restoration.

The decision to seek to redeem the relationship will usually be enhanced by seeking some professional help in dealing with all the negative emotions, and there are plenty of them. There will be anger, guilt, fear, grief, pain, disappointment, and discouragement, all on top of an undercurrent of stress that saps energy. Whether or not divorce is involved, it frequently takes months for our energy to be restored.

In no way are these suggestions made to take responsibility off erring people. Even when forgiveness is given, there will and should be consequences for those people. My point is that even with consequences decided and agreed on by all involved, divorce is no more of a deterrent to philandering than execution is to murder. Execution just assures that that murderer will not kill again. Divorce just means that a particular marriage will not have the same incidents again. Divorce is almost as irreversible as execution. Think carefully before deciding to throw the switch.

Remember that we always have choices. We can make those choices based on what we honestly think is best for us, what other people think is of little consequence. I once asked my father if he worried about what other people thought about his life. He was involved with a lot of the issues related to misconduct. He said, "If they are providing me a place to live or putting food on my table, I might think about that. If they are not doing that, I don't much care what they think." Other people do not have to deal with the day-to-day results of our decisions. They will get on with their lives regardless of what happens to us. Consider what you really want for the future and then decide.

The choice to forgive is made easier when we are able to get beyond our own egos. It is not the person who has sinned who is changed the most. Ego changes us.

I once counseled a young prostitute who wanted to stop working in her profession but was afraid that people would not let her forget. I told her that nothing was really changed in her appearance to others. There was no large P plastered on her forehead. Her sexual activity had only changed her self-perception. She could accept forgiveness and live a normal life from this day forward. Her value as a human being was still the same as everyone else's. She made the change and is now married and has a family.

I said that change is more in those around her who knew her background. "Oh, my god, your were a prostitute? How can you live with that?" The answer is that she can live with it quite well, if those of us around her set aside our own prejudice and accept her.

The same is true of one who has committed adultery. The internal change in them will be regret and guilt but their value is still as much as anyone else's. You will not be able to identify them by a big A on their foreheads. They will look like anyone else and can be like anyone else if those around them are able to forgive and accept them.

This is not intended to put the major onus on the ones hurt by the errant behavior. It is simply to say that if we want to go on with life and be redemptive, we must set aside ego and forgive. The problem of misbehavior is theirs. The problem of forgiveness is ours.

NOT TODAY

*T*he advice and observations given here are not given glibly. I have been to enough AA meetings to know that only those who have been there really understand. The old adage, "It takes one to know one," is largely true. This does not mean that only an alcoholic can help an alcoholic. It does mean that the depth of empathy is less, but help can be given. There are principles and attitudes that help, even from those who have not been there.

If you have ever been an alcoholic, I am told you will have great difficulty being in places where liquor is being served. You will find yourself drifting toward the bar without even thinking. It is a powerful addiction. People who do not understand will say that all you have to do is quit. One physician told me that is like saying to a person who has the flu, "Just don't vomit." Addictions are often too much to overcome without help and without relying on a higher power.

If you have never been addicted to gambling, you will have trouble understanding the lure of a casino, a card game, or any other game of chance. Once you win a jackpot, it is terribly tempting to return to the place of that extreme high. It is like what a professional baseball player told me about fighting the cocaine habit. He said, "It is not that it is so physically addictive, it is just that it made me feel so good that I wanted to experience it over and over. It was the hardest thing I ever had to quit."

The same is true of any addiction, including sexual addiction. There is no way for one to explain the power of being totally accepted after they have experienced much rejection or perceived rejection. Sex itself has a powerful payoff. It is the orgasm that causes people to return to and enjoy the experience. Any addiction requires special effort and perseverance to overcome.

The advice that follows is an oversimplification of advice taken from materials concerning addictions of various types. If you are addicted to any behavior, a potential part of your healing will be in researching literature related to your specific addiction. With that disclaimer I now mention some of the elementary principles in overcoming an addiction.

This advice applies to alcoholics and problem drinkers, hard drug users and addicts, peoples who struggle with their sex drive, gossips, and addicted gamblers. If you are tempted to engage in any of these behaviors, just don't do it today. You can't quit forever, but by the grace of God you can refuse to yield to the temptation today. It will certainly be helpful if you have established a relationship with someone who understands (perhaps who has had a problem similar to yours) and ask him or her for help whenever you feel tempted.

This same advice can be applied to all our sins, bad habits, obsessions, and weaknesses. Press into your mind that for today, you will simply not do them. This is an approach that has been successfully used by AA for many years. It is called "A Day at a Time." That is all we have and, thank God, we can rise above the problems, one day at a time. We don't have to worry about tomorrow until tomorrow.

Overcoming our sins one day at a time is the only hope for any of us. Even the commitment to abstain from our habits for one day at a time will require help from our higher power. We all need the grace and strength of God in our lives to overcome our weaknesses.

It is vital that we all remember that the only way we can really hope to overcome weaknesses and sin in our lives is to helplessly surrender to God, or as AA has it, "to your higher power." The point is that we seldom can make significant change without help from a source that is greater than we are.

A paraphrase of what the Apostle Paul said of his own life is, "The things that I would not do, I find myself doing. The things I would do, I find myself not doing. Who can save me from this body of sin? I thank God, through Jesus Christ" (Romans 7: 14-25). It is clear from what he wrote here that he acknowledged his own helplessness to overcome the things that did not belong in his life.

I have experienced the same frustration, haven't you? There are times that I have said of certain things, "I will never do that." Then I find myself doing that very thing. If you have a sexual problem, you no doubt have said, "I will stop doing this." Then, confronted with the passion of a moment, you did the very thing you said you would not do.

It is because of our own frailty that we need the help of others and certainly the help of God. I believe AA is right. Acknowledge the problem. Say, "I am an alcoholic." Then confess your helplessness to overcome without the help of a higher power. In your case you might be saying, "I am sexually promiscuous, and I need help in overcoming that problem. I can't overcome without the help of God."

"'Never again' is too binding a commitment, even for the strongest among us. Our past lives were full of 'never agains' and 'won't evers,' promises that were broken before the next dawn." (From *A Day at a Time*) We just need to set our sights on one good day at a time.

I used to think that the statement, "Self-sufficiency is a godless myth," was an overstatement. I now recognize it as truth. It is truth about every human being. I can do a lot of things on my own, but I am dependent in so many ways that arrogance and pride are ludicrous. That awareness in no way absolves me from personal responsibility for the decisions and actions that I make by my own choices.

The good news is that God is always ready to forgive us and help us to rise above the things that drag us down. Our commitment to resist temptation must be on a daily basis. "Today's problems are sufficient for today. So don't worry about tomorrow" Matthew 6: 34 (NIV).

LIVING THROUGH
THE DARK DAYS

When I was going through one of the most difficult periods of my life, I picked up a book that I
had been given more than ten years earlier. It is *The
Signature of Jesus* by Brennan Manning. The chapter that jumped out at me was titled, "Celebrate the
Darkness."

*T*hat was an awesome challenge for me. I remember
literally falling on my face in prayer and asking God
to help me understand the meaning of my darkness. Even if
I brought on the darkness myself, it could still be redeemed,
and I could celebrate it. One of the lessons that I learned
during that time was that even the darkest moments in life
could bring us to new levels of meaning and faith in our lives

if we permit that to happen. We are the sum total of all our experiences, good and bad. They make us what we are today.

If I had not experienced the darkness, I would probably never have the courage to write material like this. If there is any value to what I am writing, I owe it to my experience of darkness.

Darkness occurs when we feel ashamed and guilty for our failures. When we regret deeply the wrongs we have done, we begin to feel like outcasts. It is as if we are living in a dark tunnel that seems to have no end. If you have not been there, you will have difficulty understanding what I am saying. Dark times are painful but can bring much-needed insight and ultimate healing for us. I have no desire to live through any more of them, but if they come, I will embrace them as a part of my redemption.

Dark nights are essential for personal growth. Death of ego is necessary for both the person who has failed and for the person who is forgiving the failure. When I die to my selfish desires and put life in order, it is a dark night, but it leads to joy in the morning. When I die to the arrogance that will not permit me to forgive someone who has wronged me or has just done what I deem as wrong, that is a dark night. It is essential.

Manning writes, "Biblically there is nothing more detestable than a self-sufficient person. He is so full of himself, so swollen with pride and conceit that he is insufferable." Remember the biblical story of the man who thanked God that he was not like other men, especially the poor sinner in his presence. That arrogance blocks us from denying ourselves our desires, and it restrains us from forgiving others.

We are to learn from our experiences. Manning says that dark or painful experience brings on humility, an essential for healthy spiritual living. "The school of humiliation is a great learning experience; there is no other like it. When the gift of a humble heart is granted, we are more accepting of ourselves and less critical of others." He further states that, "Self-knowledge brings a humble and realistic awareness of our limitations."

If all people learn from their painful moments to be more humble, all will become more compassionate and patient with others. As much as I dislike painful experiences, I have had to admit that without those experiences my own growth in faith would have been critically stunted. I don't look forward to pain, but when it comes (and it will) I pray for the wisdom to persevere and learn from that time.

I have experienced many dark days in my life. The most difficult of those days are the ones that crash down on us personally. The day I was served with divorce papers was a dark day for me. (That same day, my father suffered a stroke that ultimately took his life.) I was a year in recovering energy after that. I don't mean to be glib about it, but I honestly look back on it as just one of the clouds that make the sunsets more beautiful. Let me explain.

It was that day, coupled with a day that I was sued by a woman who claimed to be a client of mine, that drove me to a point of great despair. My marriage had failed. I was publicly embarrassed. There were times I fell on my face pleading for God's help. In terms alcoholics understand, I had hit the bottom. I knew that I was helpless to handle all of those days in my own strength.

That experience led me to the writing of *Fire Walking*, a book about surviving the pressures of life. Ultimately I found a relationship that has enriched my life beyond my dreams. I married my present wife ten years after those dark days. Her love has been a major part of my being able to love myself again. I read a quote from Saint Augustine that sums it up for me. He said, "Love slays what we have been, that we may be what we were not."

Don't be discouraged by the dark days. They will come, but they will also pass. When we are going through the tough times, it seems trite to think, "This too will pass." But that is a fact.

Max Lucado wrote about the end of the dark days after the crucifixion of Jesus. The resurrection meant that it was all right to dream again. He gave wonderful advice when he wrote:

The lesson? Three words. Don't give up.

Is the trail dark? Don't sit.

Is the road long? Don't stop.

Is the night black? Don't quit.

He concludes that God is watching and that He still moves stones.

If any of you read this thinking you are much better than those of us who admit that we have fallen in many ways, think on the following summary statement by Manning: "Here is the final repudiation of ego. We surrender the need for vindication, hand over the kingdom of self to the Father, and in the sovereign freedom of forgiving our enemies, celebrate the luminous darkness."

Remember the caution, "There but for the grace of God, go I."

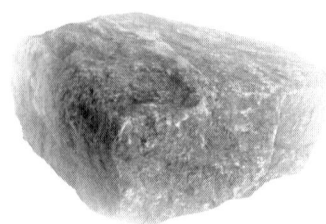

ADVICE TO THOSE WHO HAVE EXPERIENCED MISCONDUCT

*W*hen I give advice, I give a disclaimer with it. I do not claim to know that all the advice I share will apply to everyone. Read and think. When I was an active pastor, I repeatedly told the congregation that I was stating my own beliefs. They would have to determine their beliefs for themselves. Some of the things I share seem to work for me. Think about them and apply those that seem to fit you.

Self-Disclosure?

Facing the reality of our own behavior may be difficult. I am not suggesting that any of us must disclose details of our sins to others. It is probably enough to simply and honestly confess that we are sinners. Often it is hard enough to face my failures myself. It is very hard to confess them to others, but I will not pretend that no failures exist. They do.

One of the challenges that I faced in writing this material was that I am becoming more specific about my own shortcomings than I ever have. It is a scary thing to do for several reasons. For one thing there will be people close to me who may be embarrassed by my admissions. That is a risk that I think is worth taking.

My hope is that readers who struggle with some of the issues that have plagued me will find the courage to at least admit those struggles to themselves and to God. Most of us are very good at not only concealing our failures from others but also at hiding them from ourselves. It is not until we can admit to our own problems that we are getting ready to be healed.

Once I faced the problems in my life, I went into a year of professional counseling. It was a time for me to be brutally honest with myself and another human being. I found that to be wonderfully freeing. If you cannot bring yourself to seeing a professional, I recommend that you establish a confidential relationship with a trusted friend.

For most of us, it is important to set aside our pride and the arrogance that says, "I can handle this myself. All I have to do is pray and determine that I will do better." It was important for me to submit to psychological testing and receive the help mentioned above. For good measure, I also took a course in the ethics of counseling. It would seem wise to me if these were things that were included in seminary education and certainly required for people in helping professions.

You may never have a need to go public with any of your private issues. It seldom helps to spread your problems into the lives of others. That may become necessary only if there are a number of people who are already aware of your particular situation.

Stop what you are doing

Continuing in the same behavior and believing there is nothing wrong with doing so will not work. You are surely familiar with the saying, "Insanity is doing the same things in the same way over and over and expecting different results." Until we modify our personal behavior, we will continue to have the same problems.

Modifying personal behavior will require different approaches for different people. One of the things that helps me is to keep a daily journal. (Sometimes it is more like journal of every few days, but the intent is to persist in keeping it.) When I write with honesty and openness, I see in written form things that I want to change by the grace of God. If my journal reads the same at the end of a year that it did at the beginning of the year, I assume that I am not growing.

It also helps me to find reading material that speaks to my needs. I have read and re-read Manning's *The Signature of Jesus.* It has helped me through some tough times. I am not a theological conservative, but I find some conservative writings that really help me. I have read and re-read Charles Swindoll's *Grace Awakening.* I strongly recommend those two books.

I read and re-read the "Sermon on the Mount" from Matthew, chapters five, six, and seven. That is one of the most powerful sections of scripture that I know. Jesus in this sermon raises the standard of behavior from externals to internals. Not only are we not to commit murder, we are not to become angry with one another. Not only are we not to commit adultery, but also we are not to look with lust. Once we become aware that outward behavior comes from our internal beliefs and thoughts, we are in a position to examine those beliefs with a view toward changing them.

It is usually helpful to write out goals. What I mean by this is that you will benefit from becoming specific about thoughts, attitudes, and behaviors you want to change. Again, if you look back at your lists in a few months and they are not changing, redouble your efforts and get some help.

Establish some healthy rituals. There are a few things that I do every day. I pray every evening and every morning. For a year now, I have prayed the child's prayer, "Now I lay me down to sleep. I pray the Lord my soul to keep. If I should die before I wake, I pray the Lord my soul to take. If I should live another day, I pray the Lord to guide my way." I follow this with the "Lord's Prayer," and then I pray my personal prayers.

One form that is helpful for me is to ask, seek, and knock. I used those words from the Bible to ask for specific things, seek guidance, and knock for opportunities to grow and serve. There is nothing magic about this formula, and I may not be using it in another month or so, but I will use something.

Fill your mind with positive, healthy, encouraging, and pure thoughts. Write out a list of thoughts that you would like to have in your innermost belief system. Memorize them and repeat them to yourself often. "I am growing in my ability to live in accordance to my best self."

One use for positive thoughts once they are memorized is to stop yourself when you become aware of a negative thought and consciously replace that thought with a counter and positive thought. Some call this cognitive restructuring. Find material that specifically helps train your mind. "It is out of our hearts that our behaviors come."

Thoughts are the roots. My life is the tree. My deeds and words are the fruit. The better the seed, the better the fruit. So plant positive seeds in your mind every day. Do it deliberately through reading and through repeating your own list of positives.

Persevere. There is no place for us to stop growing and changing. Be diligent each day. Being useful in life depends on our own commitments. I want to be an encouraging person who spreads positive thoughts like Johnny spread apple seed.

Look on the positive side of your problem. According to Glenn Clark (author of *I Will Lift Up Mine Eyes*), the sexual desire "springs from the craving for oneness, the earthly manifestation of the most celestial and purest of all aspirations given to man." That desire can be perverted and become a wedge that separates rather than achieving oneness. Even our highest motivations can find degrading manifestation when given the wrong expression.

There are certainly times when the desire for sex is simply lust and an expression of selfishness. There is another side to that. My point is that if we can find a positive side to this problem, we may be able to prayerfully turn it around. Convert it!

Almost all sin is a perverted desire for something good. Lying is the perversion of a desire for a better or more acceptable world. It is also a perversion of our desire for acceptance. When we are afraid we will not be accepted for who we really are or what we have really done, we may make up lies to present ourselves more favorably.

Another example is stealing. While there are selfish and impure motives in many cases, there are times when stealing is a misuse of a desire for abundance. I am simply saying that if we can find the positive expression of these sins, it will help us in overcoming them.

There are therapists who recommend telling many people about your misbehavior. That seems to me to be a mistake for two reasons. Unless they are intimately involved with you, it is none of their business. If one is not careful, he or she will begin to enjoy telling people their story.

An even more compelling reason for not sharing indiscriminately is that few people will understand. When a friend of mine began to experience some deep spiritual moments in his life, I advised him to be selective in choosing those with whom he shared. Some will simply not understand and can easily dampen your enthusiasm. Share with people you trust to understand and to be supportive.

Accept your responsibility for what you have done. It is vital for your own emotional and spiritual health that you accept responsibility. We have created in America a victim mentality. Psychology has gradually found rationalizations for almost any behavior we commit. We do ourselves no favors by assuming the role of victim. Each of us must eventually be responsible for ourselves.

Some people blame their parents for their problems. Others blame society, television, and reading material, and still others blame authority figures in their lives who let them down. The bottom line is that we are wise to find the truth about our own choices. The greatest freedom in the world may be the freedom to pause before decisions and make a choice. I am responsible for my choices and so are you. Accept it and move on.

Accept responsibility and share discretely. That same advice would apply to any private behavior. That includes sexual activity, especially improper sexual activity. If you share indiscriminately, you will leave a wake of suspicion, distrust, and disappointment in them and discouragement in yourself. It is not always essential to share with anyone, but when it is important, share only with the very closest and most intimate people in your life. Don't expand the darkness.

If you have made it through dark crises and experienced understanding and forgiveness, you have received grace. If we have asked for forgiveness for past sins, we have received it. We have grace. We have forgiveness. Live like it!

ADVICE TO THOSE WHO ARE RELUCTANT TO FORGIVE

*T*here are, no doubt, many good people who will believe that I am pushing this forgiveness thing too far. It may seem that I am too weak on the seriousness of sin. After all, it was sin that nailed Jesus to the cross. Trust me when I tell you that I have wrestled long with my attitude toward sinners (myself excluded).

It is easier to forgive myself because I understand my own deepest desires and the reasons for my failures. I just don't understand yours. I understand and accept the failures of my own loved ones and friends, but I do not have that same level of acceptance toward people that I don't know that well. So it is likely that I will ask, "How far should we take this forgiveness thing?"

That is exactly what Simon Peter asked. Look at his question and read again the answer that Jesus gave to him.

> Then Peter came to Jesus and asked, "Lord, how many times shall I forgive my brother when he sins against me? Up to seven times?" Jesus answered, "I tell you not seven times, but seven times seventy.
>
> "Therefore, the kingdom of heaven is like a king who wanted to settle accounts with his servants. As he began the settlement, a man who owed him ten thousand talents (millions of dollars) was brought to him. Since he was not able to pay, the master ordered that he and his wife and his children and all that he had be sold to repay the debt. The servant fell on his knees before him. "Be patient with me," he begged, "and I will pay back everything." The servant's master took pity on him, canceled the debt, and let him go.
>
> But when that servant went out, he found one of his fellow servants who owed him a hundred denarii (a few dollars). He grabbed him and began to choke him. "Pay back what you owe me!" He demanded. His fellow servant fell to his knees and begged him, "Be patient with me, and I will pay you back." But he refused and had the man thrown into prison until he could pay the debt.
>
> When the other servants saw what had happened, they were greatly distressed and went and told their master everything that had happened. Then the mas-

ter called the servant in. "You wicked servant," he said, "I canceled all that debt of yours because you begged me to. Shouldn't you have had mercy on your fellow servant?" In anger his master turned him over to the jailers to be tortured, until he should pay back all he owed."

"This is how my heavenly Father will treat each of you unless you forgive your brother from your heart."

Matthew 18: 21-35 (NIV)

Jesus is saying that if we don't forgive one another, God will take back the forgiveness we have received! That is a strong statement on forgiveness.

Consider also what Jesus said at the end of what we call "The Lord's Prayer." He said, "For if you forgive men when they sin against you, your heavenly Father will also forgive you. But if you do not forgive men their sins, your Father will not forgive your sins" (Matthew 5:14, NIV).

How far did Jesus take that principle? He took it all the way to the cross, where he prayed for his persecutors: "Father, forgive them, for they do not know what they are doing" (Luke 23:34, NIV).

Some respond to the things being taught here, "Yes, but He was God. You can't expect me to be that forgiving. I am only human." Perhaps one example will be enough to brush aside that argument. A human, Stephen, was being stoned to death. The story is in Acts chapter seven. "While they were stoning him, Stephen prayed, 'Lord Jesus, receive my spirit.' Then he fell on his knees and cried out, 'Lord, do not hold this sin against them.' When he had said this, he fell asleep" (Acts 7:59-60, NIV).

I am not pushing the principle of forgiveness too far. It is not being soft on sin to have a forgiving spirit toward people, regardless of what they have done. That is not an easy thing, but it is the right thing. This in no way reduces moral standards. It simply raises the standard of mercy.

Another observation that has been hinted at above is that we all would be more likely to forgive if we placed our own sons, daughters, spouses, or ourselves in the place of others. There are people very close to me who have done some things that are clearly immoral. I have no difficulty being forgiving toward them. If we learn to love, respect, and accept one another, we will be able to be more forgiving.

When considering your own attitude toward any sin, including sexual sin, remember the teachings of Jesus. Then remember the statement by Manning, "Forgiveness is the key to everything."

Husbands, forgive your wives. Wives, forgive your husbands. Parents, forgive your children. Children, forgive your parents. Friends and coworkers, forgive one another. This is essential for maintaining our relationships with one another. This is a practical and spiritually grounded principle to be practiced by all.

Here is a vital thought about forgiving others. Harboring resentment is a terrible thing to do to yourself. Read carefully and thoughtfully the following paraphrase of a comment made by an alcoholic who was considering the pain he had suffered at the hands of others. He wanted to hurt them and punish them, as he had felt punished. Perhaps you can identify with his experience.

He said, "I came to realize that I cannot punish anyone without punishing myself. If I release my emotions by punishing someone else, even if it is justified, in punishing them it will leave behind trash of bitterness. This is the monotonous story of my life before I learned about forgiveness. In my life now, I do well to think about the long-range benefits of simply owning my emotions, naming them and releasing them." He then added that he believed the voice of God had a better chance of being heard when the shouting of his resentment had been released. There is tremendous wisdom in what he said. Think about it. Then determine to forgive anyone and everyone who has ever wronged you. It will be good for your own soul.

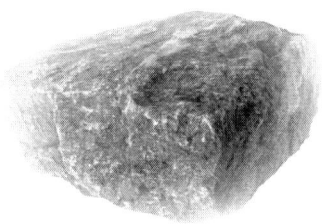

PARADISE

"Oh, for the good old days!" To hear some people talk we would be convinced that the good old days were days of heaven on earth. I do not believe that. The good old days were pretty much like the present without the conveniences. We have a better chance of living healthy lives today than ever before.

Reading history, all the way back to Abraham, convinces me that human nature has always been the same. Adultery, murder, incest, stealing, lying, arrogance, and prejudice jump out at us from the pages of history just like they do from the morning newspapers or newscasts on television.

I wish I lived in a place where no sin occurred. It would be wonderful if there were no cases of sexual misbehavior or misconduct. It would be wonderful to live in peace with all others and experience total acceptance and love. That would be paradise!

Several days after I wrote that description, it occurred to me that I could be even more specific about the meaning of paradise. Paradise would be for the kingdom of God to come on Earth as it is in heaven. On a personal level that would mean that I would not commit sin, I would not fail, and I would immediately forgive and love those who did.

The fact is that we do not live in such a place, and we still do sin and fail. We also fail to forgive and love sinners and failures. We live in a world where there are tragedies every day. People violate every commandment of God. We are all limited by our humanity. We are not perfect. This is not an excuse. It is just a fact. It is clear that we all need grace.

In such a world, we compound the tragedies by our failure to forgive and seek restoration of fallen people. Christians in general may be the guiltiest of failure in these areas that we claim to embrace. Forgiveness is like the weather. Everyone talks about it but few do anything about it. The result is that we cast aside many well-meaning, gifted, and good-hearted people because they have failures in their lives. That is more than tragic. It is catastrophic.

I cannot help wondering how many leaders like Moses we have excluded. I wonder how many Psalmists like David we have ostracized. I wonder how many spiritual leaders like Simon Peter we have excommunicated. The list goes on. My failures are on me, but forgiveness is on all of us. I hope you will at least consider the option. Forgive as you have been forgiven.

Forgiveness is like love. It can be described in glowing terms. It can be discussed in theological seminars. It can be embraced as a wonderful and right thing. But it cannot be understood until it happens to us. I don't really understand romantic love until I fall in love myself. I cannot understand what it means to forgive until someone has really hurt me, and I have walked through the experience of forgiving him or her.

I was hurt in college when the president of the school I attended decided to veto my basketball scholarship. The reason he gave was that I was a ministerial student and married. He thought I should not play basketball but find other means of paying for my education. I continued to play but was not able to practice because of part-time work. The coach was gracious and permitted me to continue on a part-time basis.

My hurt was intensified the next year when the president approved a scholarship for another married ministerial student. I grew bitter about the incident. The truth is that it was actually years before I could say that I forgave him for that unfairness. It might be hard for some to believe, but I actually lost sleep thinking about that situation until I forgave him in my heart. For the first time in a long time, I could rest without thinking about that issue.

If one could be petty about such a minor hurt, it is understandable that bigger hurts are still more difficult to forgive. But forgive we must because we do not live in paradise yet.

Paradise is a place where there is no sickness, no war, no sin, and no emotional pain, and where love, respect, and reverence characterize all relationships. That is what we are seeking when we pray for the kingdom of God to come on Earth as it is in heaven. The fact is it does not exist in this world for any extended time. That is why we must have grace and forgiveness.

I pray for paradise to come on Earth as it is in heaven. I pray that we will learn to forgive those who have hurt us as they and God forgive us. I pray that we will live in such close proximity to God that we will find the power to overcome any temptation that confronts us. You may recognize this as a paraphrase of parts of the "Lord's Prayer."

We all aspire to live in paradise, and I believe we shall, but entrance is gained only through the door of grace. Everyone, and I mean everyone, enters through the same door.

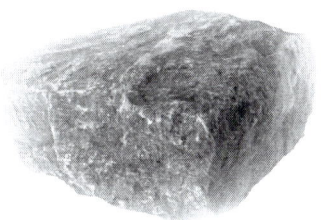

WHAT CAN WE LEARN
FROM ALL THIS?

**We can learn to receive good messages
and services from imperfect people.**

*I*t is common knowledge that we hold people to different standards because of their positions in life. We expect more from some professions than from others. We expect policemen to be honest. Some are and some are not. We expect teachers to be of higher moral standing than salesmen. Some are and some are not. We expect clergymen and clergywomen to be people who live pure lives. Some do and some do not. The fact is that the common thread tying us all together is our humanity. None of us are gods. We are human beings.

I am focusing here on religious people, but the same principles apply to all people. We are all imperfect and frequently in need of grace. I believe we are in need of grace every day. The apostle Paul, in 2 Corinthians 4:7, spoke of our common humanity. In saying that we have the message of the gospel in us (all Christians), he observed that we have this treasure in "earthen vessels." That was his way of saying that even those who share the gospel of Jesus with others have flawed lives. We are all earthen vessels.

Some will be bothered by the admission that ministers may be preaching the gospel while at the same time having a sexual affair. That is not just a guess. It is a fact. The gospel is held in imperfect containers. The living water flows through rusty pipes. It is not only sexual sins that make us imperfect vessels or rusty pipes. It is all kinds of sin. We have to deal with our own.

There are no perfect conduits for the message of God. One of the finest men I know came to me one day and said, "I am having trouble in my prayer life. I want to confess my sins and pray for forgiveness, but I can't think of any to confess."

I suggested, "Just guess at some."

He was serious in his question and asked, "What would I guess?"

I said, "You might start with spiritual pride." Even the best of us have our warts.

Does this knowledge mean that we cannot get a message from God through these imperfect messengers? I certainly hope that is not the case. If it is, we will never get such a message. The fact is that if I have a spiritual hunger, I will eat bread baked in an imperfect oven. If I have a burning thirst for eternal life, I will gladly drink living water that flows through a rusty pipe.

This is not even a thinly veiled attempt to urge giving confessed sinners a chance to pursue their callings. A discouraged person can encourage you. A divorced person can offer helpful advice for building strong marriage. Though my father would never have agreed, it is also true that you can receive healthy information and get help for your illnesses from a sick physician. The message and the benefit come not from the outward vessel but from inner knowledge, gifts, and wisdom. That is why we can be inspired by the writings of adulterous and murdering King David. He was gifted and inspired. Thank God we have his writings to teach and comfort us. I think we would have been fortunate if he had been our pastor. As we have been often warned, "Don't throw out the baby with the dirty bath water."

I Believe We Learn That If There Was More Forgiveness There Would Be More Confessions

We are not as likely to confess our sins if we do not believe there will be acceptance of us after the confession. Years ago, when smoking was only acceptable in tobacco-growing states, I was still smoking. One Sunday morning I made the following statement to the congregation.

"If anyone tells you that he or she saw me smoking, they are probably telling the truth, because I do smoke. I don't smoke a lot. I usually only smoke while I am playing cards." I was speaking to the church about being honest about who we are.

After the service a lady came up to me and said, "I am never coming to hear you preach again." I asked why and she said, "Because you said that you smoke."

I said, "But I do smoke. I was just trying to be honest about it."

She responded, "Well, you shouldn't tell people about it."

I said, "You failed the test." After she asked what I meant, I went on, "This week I decided to tell you some of my minor sins. I was going to tell you the big ones next week."

She looked at me and grinned. She never stopped attending our services for the rest of her life. My point was made in jest, but it was nevertheless true. If people can't handle confession of acceptable sins, how would they respond to unacceptable ones? I guess I never trusted the church enough to confess and seek forgiveness for major flaws.

If we expect to be a community of redemption, we will have to become less judgmental and more forgiving. We cannot get far from the need for forgiveness if we expect to help people who struggle with their lives.

We Learn That We Are Likely To Be Judged On The Basis Of Mistakes And Not On The Bulk Of Our Lives

Once people know about a failure, especially a sexual failure in our lives, they tend to forget about other things. That has not been my experience, but I understand that it is the experience of others.

I suspect I am like most other ministers. I have served one congregation as senior pastor for more than fifty-one years. During that fifty plus years, I have made thousands of visits to hospitals, nursing homes, and residences to minister to the needs of suffering people. I have preached hundreds of funerals and spent time with grieving families. I have preached more than 5,000 sermons, met with deacons, trustees, and dozens of committees, written and published ten books, and done thousands of hours of personal counseling, both on the radio and in my office. In addition, my wife, Gay, and I co-founded and ran a cancer support center for ten years, during which time we saw and helped more than 1,500 cancer patients. I never missed more than three Sundays a year in my pulpit.

During those years, I attended seminary, finished three graduate degrees, worked with two major league baseball teams, and led seminars for organizations all over this country. I also found time to make my share of mistakes and get into trouble. I recount all this to make the point that, like most others, about 99 percent of my life has been focused on doing positive things. If I am judged on the 1 percent when I was messing up, I stand no chance of being accepted.

I am thankful that I served a church that accepted me as a fallible human being and remained aware of the bulk of my work while forgiving my failures. "God bless them and may their number increase."

We Learn That We Are All Pretty Much In The Same Boat

There are exceptions, but the bulk of people in all professions mean well and do a good job with a high percentage of their time. I know this is true among the people I know. I have worked with professional athletes, with medical people, with professional people, with blue-collar workers, with students, and families of lay people. I have found that most of them are very similar in living their lives. They make mistakes but generally mean well.

There are exceptions. There are people who are hell bent on creating problems. There are people who commit atrocious acts against mates, children, and the general public, but they are the exceptions.

We Learn That There Are Consequences To Behavior

Most of us have had the good fortune to be treated more than fairly by our families and friends. We thankfully pray, "I am thankful that I have not received what I have deserved but have been really blessed." That is the prayer of one who lives as a recipient of grace.

There are situations that exceed the protective circles of grace. I have a good friend who is presently in prison. I don't know if he will ever get out, but I continue to work to find help for him. He is a man who spent most of his life defending people from criminals and serving in his church in a lot of mission projects. One night he got drunk and spent the evening with a prostitute.

He passed out, and when he awoke he thought the woman was going through his wallet. He grabbed her, and in the ensuing struggle, he choked her. She died. In a panic, he dragged her body outside and made a feeble attempt to hide it. He was given twenty years for manslaughter.

I know this man. I have roomed with him on trips when we played basketball together. I have ridden with him on some of those trips, and we have spent several hours talking about mutual spiritual interests. He knows and I know that he had to pay a consequence for what he did. I just hope that there is some mercy and forgiveness for him. He has not found that mercy with the parole board in our state, but I continue to pray for his release.

He has continued to do the best he can for almost ten years in prison. He has helped younger inmates (he is in his mid-seventies) to get their GEDs. He works with athletic programs and other educational activities and is a model prisoner, as he was a model citizen with most of his life. He regrets terribly what he did. Still there is the consequence.

At the very least, when our failures are known, we experience personal embarrassment and humiliation. If they are not known, we still experience a sense of guilt. Guilt is a trip that I do not recommend. It is a consequence of the failures in our lives. As I have repeatedly said, "If you have guilt, confess your sin and seek forgiveness through repentance and grace." That will not remove all the consequences, but it will make a tremendous and positive difference. It will, in most cases, permit a resurrection to a meaningful life.

We Learn That We All Need To Be More Understanding Of Others

Stephen Covey's excellent book *Seven Habits of Highly Successful People* challenges us to seek first to understand and then to be understood. When we understand others, our empathy for them grows, and we are less likely to be judgmental of them. We find it easier to forgive when we understand.

It is difficult for us to empathize with people we do not know. It is, on the other hand, easy to empathize with people we know and love. Before we draw conclusions about people, we would be wise to attempt to hear their side of the story.

I empathize with my friend who is in prison for manslaughter. I have never tried to justify his behavior, but I believe I understand him. He cannot change what he did, but he can make positive contributions to others even now. I hurt with the family of the woman he killed. I also hurt with him and did so when he was unable to attend the funeral of his daughter.

Understanding does not mean approval, but it does mean an increase in our ability to accept and forgive others in the same way we all hope we will be accepted and forgiven. Seek first to understand.

We Learn That All People Are Useful In The Kingdom Of God If They Desire To Be

A valuable lesson for all who attempt to serve God is that none of us have fallen so low or become so bad that God cannot use us. I cling to that truth and thank God that He loves me—warts and all. This is an essential message to all us imperfect people.

Divorced people, publicly disgraced people, confessed criminals, adulterers, drug addicts, and all other outcasts can take heart in the fact that the Gospel of Jesus Christ does not reject them from serving him. This is not to justify our failures but simply to confess them and accept the grace of God.

Starr Daily was a murderer. He was in prison for that crime serving a life sentence when he experienced forgiveness from God. He was ultimately released from prison and became a teacher of prayer. He spoke on many university campuses and in churches all over the world. He made a great contribution to the kingdom of God. He was evidence that even fallen human beings can make contributions to our lives. Thank God that is true or none of us would be able to serve in positive ways.

We Surely Learn That We Cannot Change What We Have Already Done

I have a friend who started playing golf fairly late in life. We play together a lot. When he first started, when he hit a bad shot he would say, "I can do better than that." Then he would take another shot.

In life we do not get do overs. It is important that we get it right as early as possible.

Life is uncomfortably short. We do not have time to continue making the same mistakes over and over again. When a page of our history is written, it is written. We cannot undo one thing from our past. Beginning now to do it right is vital.

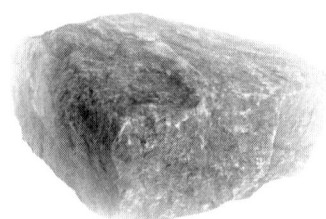

FINAL THOUGHTS AND CONCLUSION

*A*mericans have been given abundance. We are, with all our struggles, still one of the richest nations ever to exist. Because we have had so much, we have had a tendency to waste. We throw away things that could be useful.

One of my worst sins is the sin of wasted opportunity. I have wasted money. I have wasted time. I have wasted opportunities to do things that I regret not having done. When I look back at my life, I believe that I will be pleased with many of my accomplishments, but I will look with grief at the things I could have done. I know we are all aware of the tragic statement from Whittier, "For of all sad words of tongue and pen, the saddest are these: 'It might have been!'"

The realization that I have wasted so much motivates me to make the best use of what I have right now. I suppose part of that is a function of my age. As we get closer and closer to the end of life, we become aware of the importance of putting forth more effort to get things done.

As I write this material, I write with a hope that it will at least stop some from wasting the good that could be done. Those of us who were aware of the presidency of Bill Clinton observed a brilliant man and exceptional leader who almost wasted his great opportunity. There were many who believed that he should not have continued as president after the sexual misbehavior in his life. I am glad that that mistake was not compounded by failure to permit him to continue. He turned out to be a very good president and continues to make positive contributions to our society in the years after his oval office years ended.

In my mind that is analogous to wasting the lives of gifted men and women in other areas of life, including ministry. When people fall short of our expectations, we are apt to become so disappointed that we fail to give them any chance to continue service. Of course, if a person stubbornly continues to follow a destructive course of living, there must be a limit.

People who have been given repeated chances to succeed and continue to pursue selfish desires at the expense of morality cannot be permitted to continue without getting some kind of professional help. Perhaps a year off and a demand that such people spend a year in therapy is a possible direction. I know that in the Catholic Church priests have been placed in rehab centers to help them deal with their abnormalities. That is an attempt at corrective action.

For me the bottom line is not to lower the standards of morality but to raise the standards of benevolent, compassionate, and forgiving attitudes. Jesus did not tell the woman who was caught in adultery that she did nothing wrong. He did tell her that he did not condemn her and instructed her to stop such behavior. That is compassion, and I believe it is effective in helping people overcome their weaknesses and sin.

Discouragement is one of the worst culprits in our world. When children are discouraged, they tend to misbehave. When adults are discouraged, they resort to childish reactions and misbehave. I believe that discouraged people commit most crimes. Abused children become abusers. People who have been beaten down often rebel against authority. This observation is not to justify misbehavior but to suggest that we might avoid a lot of destructive behaviors if we were more encouraging to one another. I often quote the statement, "No one ever died from an overdose of encouragement." I will repeat it at the end of this book. We are never reminded too often to be encouraging people.

Unless we generate more acceptance and forgiveness, we will continue to waste lives and discourage people. If we want a better world and fewer personal failures, we will become more encouraging to those who admittedly have fallen short of the best standards. I thank God for the letters and calls I have received from supportive people when I have faced my own failures.

I visited a widow woman who was in her nineties. She met me with a smile and told me, "No matter what has happened, I want you to know that I believe in you and love you." She gave me a boost that continues to impact my life in a positive way. Encouragement like that makes me want more than ever to do the very best I can with my life. It is more motivating than a thousand lectures on morality.

When I told my wife of accusations that were made toward me she said, "I just want you to know that regardless of what happened I am with you, and I love you." Those words and that sentiment have strengthened me in some of my darkest moments. She may never know just how much it meant. I thank God for her and for people like the woman I mentioned above.

I have received dozens of cards and some letters from people with the message "Don't give up. We love you and appreciate all that you have done for us." That message was repeated in most of the notes, cards, and letters that I received after my retirement. Those love notes have motivated me to look for ways to do more for them and for others. They are one of the reasons that I continue to write.

When I hear of a minister who is going through a public humiliation because of a moral failure, sexual or otherwise, I either contact him or her personally or contact people who know them. I urge their friends to call, visit, or write with words of compassion, forgiveness, and encouragement to them. That will be redemptive.

Well-meaning people have said things that make it more difficult for me to extend grace to others and to receive it for myself. A seminary professor I respected and loved very much once said to one of our classes, "If a minister ever gets involved in sexual misbehavior, he will never be worth anything after that."

With the passing of time, I realize he was wrong. He never said, "If a minister becomes too full of himself and is arrogant, he will never be worth anything after that." He never said, "If a minister ever lies to his congregation, he will never be worth anything after that." It would be equally wrong to make any of those statements. The fact is that we can always be worth as much as anyone else if we just pick up the pieces and go on.

Some will not respond to the encouragement but others will. Since we do not know who will do what, we can be generous in our support to all and let them become responsible for their own responses. I am not responsible for how you respond to my acceptance of you, but I am responsible for accepting you.

Conclusion: When Sinners Repent They Are Forgiven. Here Is The Most Relevant Question To Be Considered

The question that should be relevant to all Christians is, "What would Jesus do?" I once had a conversation with a friend about attitudes toward war, and I asked him that question. His answer was, "Jesus doesn't have anything to do with it. He was God, and we are only human." I do not agree. The attitude of Jesus is to be considered in any issue we face.

I can imagine a scene something like this. Denominational leaders, followed by many laymen, come to Jesus leading a minister who had been caught in sexual misconduct. They say to Jesus, "This man was caught in sexual misconduct. According to our codes, we plan to vote him out of our fellowship and make him a ministerial outcast. What do you say?"

Jesus, after an uncomfortable pause, says, "Let those among you who have no sin cast the first votes." Soon only the embarrassed minister is standing alone before Jesus because the accusers have, one by one, drifted away.

I can imagine further that Jesus looks at the man and says, 'Where are they? Has no one voted to make you an outcast?'

The minister responds, 'No, Lord. No one has voted to cast me out."

Jesus says, "Neither do I condemn you or cast you out. Go and sin no more, but continue to feed my sheep.'"

Is that a fair representation of the attitude of Jesus? Is it your attitude? Christians must examine our own attitudes in the light of the nature and character of Jesus. "What would Jesus do?" is always a relevant question and should govern our attitudes. It should govern the attitudes of husbands and wives. It should govern the attitude of all of us in our reactions to the behaviors of others. Every sin is forgivable before God.

EPILOGUE

*I*t is fitting for me to close every seminar I do with a comment I heard years ago. "Encourage one another. Remember that no one ever died from an overdose of encouragement." So I close with this notation that I hope is a word of encouragement to the readers.

No matter what has happened in your past, be of good courage and persevere.

BIBLIOGRAPHY

"A Day At A Time," (CompCare Publications, Minneapolis, Minn. 1976)

Clark, Glenn, "I Will Lift Up Mine Eyes" Harper & Row, Publishers, New York, NY, 1937)

Lacado, Max, "He Still Moves Stones" (Word Publishers, Dallas, TX, 1993)

Little, Bill, "Fire Walking" (Peake Road, Macon, GA, 1997)

Manning, Brennan, "The Signature of Jesus" (Multnomah, Portland, Oregon, 1992)

Swindoll, Charles, "Grace Awakening" (Word Publishing, Dallas TX, 1990)

Young, Wm. Paul, "The Shack" (Windblown Media, Newbury Park, CA, 2007)